COMPUTERS
THOSE AMAZING MACHINES

by Catherine O'Neill

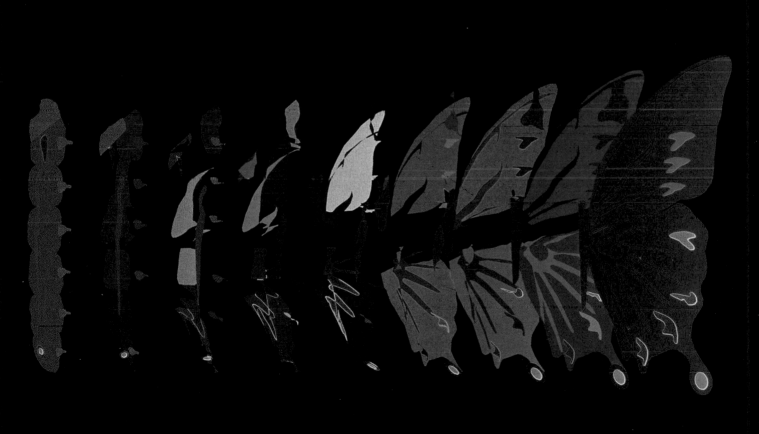

BOOKS FOR WORLD EXPLORERS
NATIONAL GEOGRAPHIC SOCIETY

CONTENTS

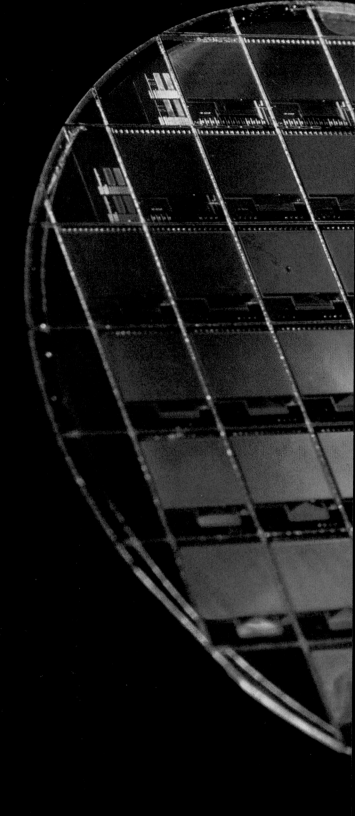

COVER: *Tiny powerhouse. The chip—a piece of electronic equipment small enough to rest in your palm—makes it possible for computers to accomplish the amazing things they do today.*
KEN COOPER/THE IMAGE BANK

TITLE PAGE: *A computer program called IN-BETWEENING produced this artistic image of a caterpillar's metamorphosis—change of form—into a butterfly. The artist entered just the caterpillar and the complete butterfly. The program filled in the middle "stages."*
MIKE NEWMAN/DICOMED CORPORATION

A wafer only 2 inches (5 cm)* across (right) holds 48 computer chips. Each chip, known as a bubble memory chip, stores enormous amounts of coded information.
DAN MCCOY/RAINBOW

*Metric figures in this book have been rounded off.

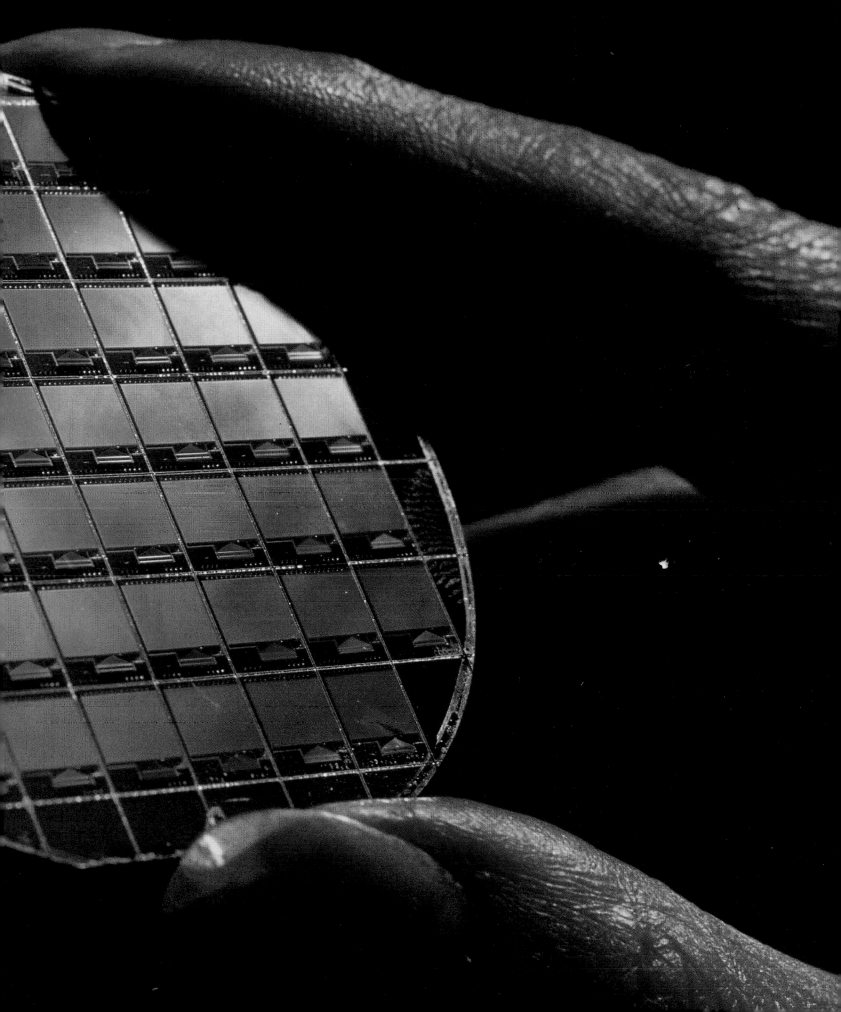

INTRODUCTION

Nowadays it's not unusual to hear conversations loaded with such words as "input" and "output," "software" and "hardware," and "bits" and "bytes." You could hear them used by engineers in a factory or by fourth graders on a playground. They might be used by farmers or doctors or artists. They all have to do with computers. As you read this book, you'll become familiar with these computer words—and more.

Just what is a computer? It's a machine that can accept instructions, store information, decide what the information means, and then act on it—either by flashing the results on a screen or by doing a task.

Computers are just about everywhere. They're in your classroom, in your doctor's office, and perhaps in your wristwatch. Computers read to the blind, cook food, and even set the stage for a rock concert. In Chapter 1, you'll see some familiar uses for computers—and discover some new ones, too.

As machines go, computers are a fairly recent development. Even so, they have changed amazingly fast. When the first general-purpose electronic computer was put into use, in the 1940s, it filled a room the size of a house. Today, a computer chip smaller than your fingernail can perform 200 times as many calculations a second as that huge machine did. Called a chip because it's so small, this essential piece of equipment contains a complex set of switches to control the flow of electricity through its circuits. Computers use electricity to do their many jobs, and they work fast. In one second, a computer can do an amount of arithmetic that would keep 20 people busy all day.

At the beginning of the computer age, only trained scientists could operate the machines. Today, children use them to learn foreign languages and spelling, to draw pictures, and to write stories. Every summer, young computer enthusiasts flock to camps where they learn more about computers. The campers may play a lot of video games, but first they must create them—and program the camp's computers to play them.

"Programming" means communicating with a computer in ways that it—and you—can understand. Using a code of letters, numbers, and symbols called a programming language, you tell the computer what to do and how to do it. The machine changes the letters, numbers, and symbols into electrical pulses—its language. These pulses flash

Turtle tracks. Christopher McCoy, 10, watches a device called a Tasman Turtle draw a design (right). Christopher, who lives in Housatonic, Massachusetts, found out how to communicate with the Turtle at computer camp. He learned LOGO, a simple programming language. Then he typed a set of LOGO instructions—a program—into a computer. His program tells the Turtle what lines and angles to draw and where to draw them.

through the circuits as the computer carries out your program. You'll learn more about how computers work in Chapter 2.

Computers have changed the way many people do their jobs. Writers use word-processing programs to compose stories on computers. Office computer systems have freed many people to work on more flexible schedules or even to work at home.

Many manufacturers use computerized workers called robots to do jobs once done by people. A leading car maker, the General Motors Corporation, recently announced plans for a computerized factory where robots will even sweep the floors. You'll see factory robots in action in Chapter 3.

Already, computers are programmed to prepare paychecks, send bills, keep medical records, design cars, and help send people into space. What will they do in the future? In Chapter 4, you'll find out that one day computers may run your house, grow your food, and operate the factories where the products you use are made.

Some people worry that robotics—the science of designing and building robots to do work—is taking jobs away from people. Others argue that the electronics industry is creating new jobs. Who is right? You can decide for yourself after you read about careers in computing, at the end of Chapter 4.

Computers *are* amazing machines. Even so, computer whizzes have a favorite expression they often use. It's "GIGO," (GIH-go) a made-up word that stands for "garbage in, garbage out." That word reminds computer users that the machines are only as useful as the programs people write for them.

Outdoor office. In a mountain meadow near Aspen, Colorado, Steve Roberts writes an article on his solar-powered portable computer (above). Roberts rode his bicycle around the United States, writing stories as he went. He sent his work to magazines and newspapers over regular telephone lines. He hooked his computer to one end of the line; a computer on the other end received the message.

"Now add sugar." To bake a cake, a woman follows a recipe on the television screen in her kitchen (left), in Los Angeles, California. She subscribes to a type of information service called videotex. A cable hookup transforms her TV into the display terminal of a far-off computer containing a data base. The data base is crammed with useful information, from recipes to weather reports.

Stay tuned. At "switching central" at NBC television, in New York City, technical directors watch many shows at once (below). They use computers to control the timing of the programs and commercials shown on NBC.

Rows of robots fill a room at Androbot, Inc., a company in San Jose, California (right). These machines, all named Topo, are controlled by computers. They can be programmed to deliver snacks, sing songs, play question-and-answer games, or tell jokes.

Bedside manner. A robot invented at Tokyo University, in Japan, answers a bedridden patient's command to pour a drink (below). Then the computerized arms deliver the drink to the patient. Eighteen motors—three in each hand and six in each arm—enable this machine to perform many nursing tasks.

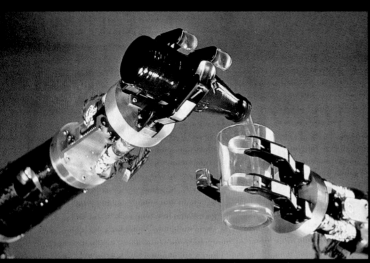

COMPUTERS IN EVERYDAY LIFE

Computerized concert. Michael Jackson puts on an electrifying performance during the Jacksons' 1984 Victory Tour. As Jackson sang, computers controlled many of the show's special effects. One computer made a pair of robot spiders wriggle as the band performed. Another computer directed a laser-light show. Four additional computers worked the lighting and sound systems.

DENNIS HAMILTON, JR./LGI

When the Jacksons' musical group loaded more than a dozen trucks with equipment to go on the road with their Victory Tour, in 1984, they took their computers along . . . and not just for making music. "The most difficult part of the tour was making sure everything fit together," says Peyton Wilson, production manager of the tour. "We all needed computers just to communicate with each other."

Computers are amazingly adaptable machines. People can program them to play music out loud or to print musical notes on paper. Computers can tell mechanical spiders when to move—as they did during the Jacksons' stage show. They can tell a mechanical

hand to open or close—or even to play an organ.

Computers haven't been around long, but people already have learned many uses for them. Some of the uses are strictly educational; some are pure fun. Computers make life easier for people with special needs, such as the blind and the deaf. Computers entertain us, help us take care of our homes, and help creative people practice their arts.

If you could visit jazz musician Herbie Hancock's home studio, in Hollywood, California, you'd find several keyboard instruments attached to computers. Hancock uses the computers when he composes music. He may start out with familiar sounds such as piano notes, but with his computer equipment he changes the tones electronically until they sound like something you've never heard before.

Very complex computer instruments allow a single musician to sound like an entire orchestra. Randy Jackson did that during the Victory Tour. He played only one keyboard—but it was attached to 11 machines called synthesizers (SIN-thuh-sye-zers), that could make sounds ranging from wailing horns to jangling marimbas (muh-RIM-buhz).

Some computer instruments available for use at home play one part of a piece while you play another. Others supply a driving drum rhythm while you

One-man band. Jazz musician Herbie Hancock (left) makes music in the studio of his home in Hollywood, California. The instruments around him are attached to computers that make one keyboard sound like an entire orchestra, even though only one person's fingers hit the keys.

Using a device called a synthesizer, Max Mathews adjusts a musical tone (below). Mathews was the first person to use computers to play music. Computer sounds can resemble musical instruments, voices—or something from another world.

play a melody. Some of the instruments record your music as you play. Push a button, and you hear an instant replay of your performance.

How do computers make music? They process a stream of numbers that represent, or stand for, sound waves. You probably know that all sounds are created by vibrations in the air. The shape of that vibration is called a waveform. A computer converts, or changes, waveforms into numbers that travel through the computer's circuits the same way words and other numbers do—as electrical pulses.

To start your piece of computerized music, you either type out codes or punch keys that represent musical notes. The computer then sends pulses representing the numbered waveform of each note to a synthesizer. The synthesizer may take the form of a chip inside the computer, or it may be an accessory attached to it. The synthesizer then converts the pulses into sounds.

Seem complicated? It is. But the transformation from keyboard to number to sound takes place remarkably fast, and allows musicians much freedom. Change the numbers a little, and a piano sound turns into a violin sound. Change the numbers a little more, and the violins may sound like piccolos—or like the sound effects used in video games.

Synthesizers produce sounds like those of just about any instrument you can think of, including a grand piano. But synthesizers also produce sounds that aren't musical. One example is the *beep-beep* produced by a touch-tone telephone.

For musicians and music lovers, computers can be fun. A Japanese inventor even programmed a robot to play the organ—although the work took several years and cost more than a million dollars. Computer

High-tech duet. Japanese professor of engineering Ichiro Kato performs with WAM-7, an organ-playing robot he designed. The robot is programmed to hit the keys with its hinged fingers. Like a human, WAM-7 can cross one finger over another for correct fingering. This robot is more than a gimmick. The technology it demonstrates can help scientists as they work to build better artificial arms and hands.

15

signals tell the robot, named WAM-7, what notes to play with its metal manipulators, or fingers.

WAM-7 and the later WABOT 2—a robot capable of even more wrist and finger movement—are entertaining machines. But they're more than just gadgets. The delicate pieces of wire and metal that enable the robots to play anything from Bach to rock may someday help disabled people lead more normal lives.

Ichiro Kato, the inventor of WAM-7 and WABOT 2, is known as the father of robotics in Japan. In addition to his musical robots, Dr. Kato has invented a walking machine with good foot and ankle action. The walking machine moves more like a human leg than most artificial limbs do.

In many parts of the world, talented inventors are hard at work developing better and better robots. The Japanese government, for example, has set aside a large amount of money—about 88 million dollars—for a research program to develop computer-driven robots. The project will be complete in 1991. Can you imagine what kinds of robots the inventors will have designed by then?

Today, computers have already improved the lives of many people with special needs. The deaf can use home computers hooked up to modems to relay printed messages. Modems are devices that let one

Playing the piano is one of Christa Bevilacqua's favorite hobbies—even though she was born without a left hand. Christa, 12, of Wenonah, New Jersey, uses her myoelectric (my-oh-lh-LEK-trik) hand (below) to play the low notes. The device gets its name from "myo," a Greek word for muscle, plus "electric." When Christa tenses muscles in her arm, electric signals travel to circuits in the myoelectric hand. Switches inside the hand then command it to open or close.

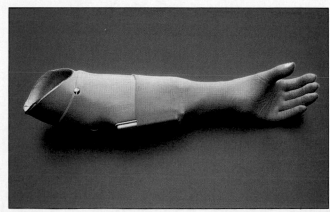

computer communicate with other computers by way of the telephone. Many blind people depend on home computers equipped with sound synthesizers to listen to information they can't read on a printout or a monitor—a kind of TV screen. For people who can't move around easily, home computers offer an instant link to the office. Workers with disabilities can hold productive jobs without having to leave home at all.

Christa Bevilacqua's myoelectric hand, shown here and on pages 16 and 17, uses small electronic parts to operate. Before she got the new hand, Christa, who lives in Wenonah, New Jersey, used a metal hook attached to her body with a harness. Her new hand fits easily onto her arm. Wearing it is less tiring than the hook was. Her myoelectric hand also has a better grip than a hook does. It allows more control for favorite sports such as tennis or softball.

Myoelectric replacement parts, such as arms, hands, and legs, aren't perfect. Wearers often must spend many hours training their muscles to send the right signals to the electronic parts that tell a hand to open or close or a leg to bend. For people who need them, myoelectric limbs open up a whole new world. They give their wearers freedom to ride bikes, dress themselves, play on swings—even climb trees.

Freedom of movement can mean a lot to disabled people. Many blind people depend on guide dogs to lead them along crowded streets. In Japan, scientists are working on a computerized version of the guide dog. It has a map in its memory, and can chart routes to and from places within the mapped area.

For several years now, the blind have also used computers for reading. You may have noticed blind students using devices called VersaBraille (VUR-suh-BRAYL) machines. With these computers, blind people can take notes in Braille, a kind of writing that uses raised dots instead of (Continued on page 22)

Using her myoelectric hand, Christa tosses a racquetball into the air. Her brother, Danny, 10, waits to receive the serve. The artificial hand has a stronger grip than the metal hook Christa used to wear, making sports more enjoyable. "The myoelectric hand makes everyday activities much easier, and it is more normal in appearance," says Christa.

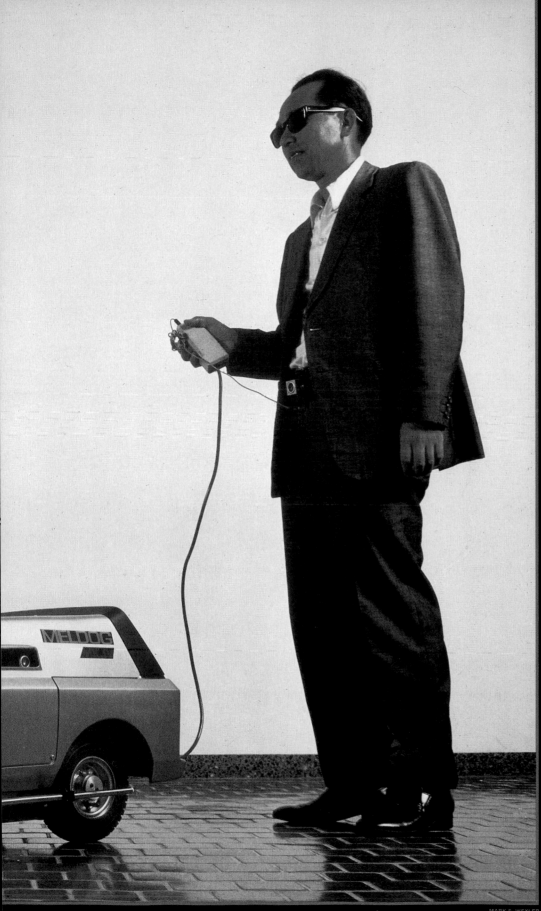

Meet Meldog. A "blind" man and a guide dog, left, encounter an experimental guide robot. Meldog, the robot, is leading Kenji Miyamura, a teacher at a school for the blind in Japan. With the real dog is Susumu Tachi, Meldog's inventor. Dr. Tachi is a scientist from the Mechanical Engineering Laboratory, in Ibaraki, Japan. Scientists at the lab used computers and robot technology to build Meldog. The robot's computer memory contains a map of an area. When a user tells Meldog to go to a place within that area, Meldog charts a route to follow. As the robot moves, it senses when something is in its way and avoids it by stopping or by turning in another direction. The robot lets its user know what's happening through a system of mild electrical buzzes that can be felt on the skin.

(Continued from page 18) letters. The VersaBraille machine records what is typed into it. It also can display the information later in lines of Braille.

In the United States, only about one blind person in every ten knows Braille. For those who don't know the system, a reading machine invented by a computer expert named Ray Kurzweil may be very useful.

The Kurzweil Reading Machine takes an electronic picture of words on a page. Then a computer identifies the letters, groups them into words, and transmits the words to a synthesizer, which reads them aloud. The machine can read almost any printed material. Many libraries have installed the machines.

At her home, in San Francisco, California, Michela Alioto uses a personal computer made by Apple. Michela, 17, was disabled in a skiing accident and must get around by wheelchair. For her, the computer provides hours of entertainment—and it helps her with homework, too. She slips word-processing or game programs into her computer and keeps track of how many math problems she has completed—or the number of space invaders she has zapped.

Computers play an even greater role in Michela's life than with games and at school. At a clinic, using the same kind of Apple hardware, or machine, Michela's physical therapist helps her keep her muscles in shape. You can see her working with Michela in the photograph at right. The therapist uses software—programs—that tell the computer how to run the exercises, or how to measure Michela's heart rate or count the number of exercises she does.

Back in the 1950s, scientists at Brookhaven, a research laboratory in New York State, invented what probably was the first video game ever. It was a simple game—players just batted a dot back and forth across a line on the screen of a scientific instrument called an oscilloscope. That early game is the

---

At a university library in Washington, D. C., Janean Chambers, a D. C. Vision Program student, listens to a book (below). Janean, who is blind, uses the Kurzweil Reading Machine. The machine contains a camera that sends an image of letters on a page to a computer. The computer recognizes the letters one by one, and groups them into words. Another microprocessor converts the words into sounds spoken by a synthesized voice.

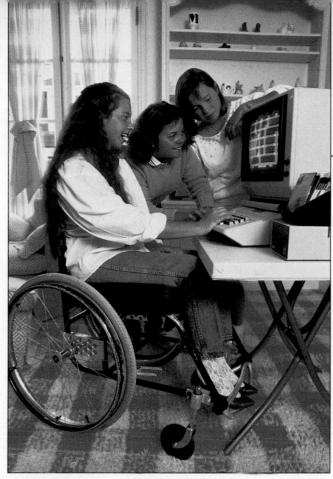

At home, Michela Alioto, 17, of San Francisco, California, plays a game on an Apple II+ personal computer (left). Her sister Angelina, 16, right, and cousin Anne Farrah, 17, cheer her on. Michela was injured in a skiing accident at age 12.

At a clinic, another Apple II+ computer helps a physical therapist keep Michela's muscles healthy (below). Through sensors taped to Michela's legs, the computer sends pulses to her muscles, making them move. If her spinal injury can ever be repaired, Michela's muscles will be strong enough to support her.

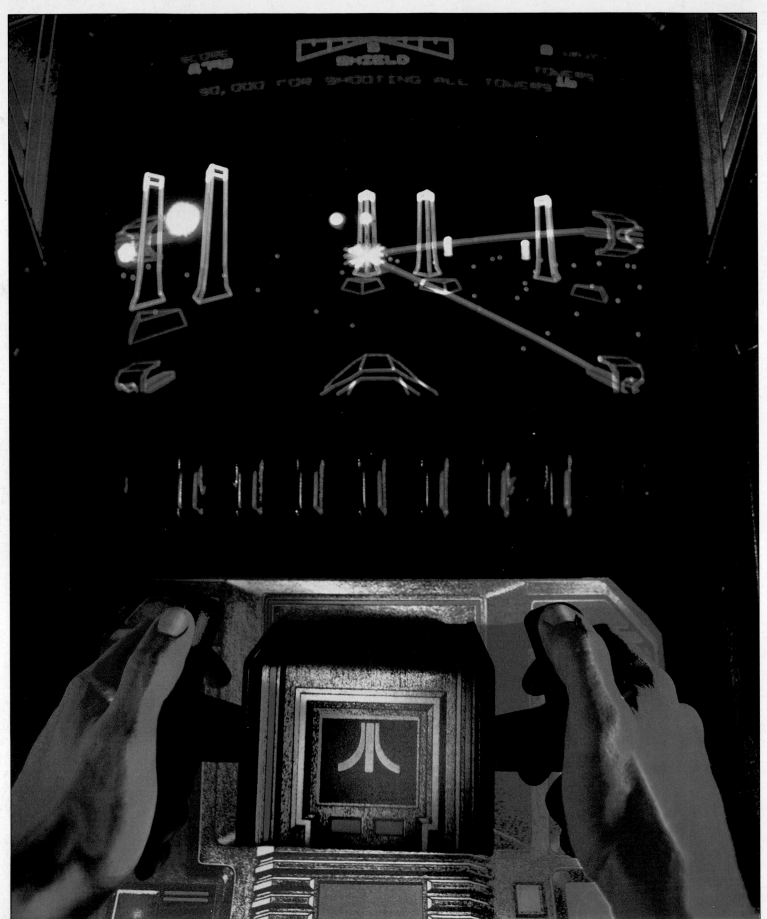

50,000 FOR SHOOTING ALL TOWERS

SHIELD

Video pilot. Using an Atari video game to play STAR WARS, a player sends Luke Skywalker's X-WING FIGHTER zooming through an obstacle course (left). Since video games were introduced in the 1970s, those played in arcades as well as the home variety have been popular amusements. Through them, players often discover the excitement of creating their own computer programs.

Championship play. Video game experts and onlookers crowd a contest organized to raise money for the Massachusetts Association for Mental Health (below). Thousands of people from the Boston area took part in the event. Five hundred finalists, from fourth graders to adults, were in the play-offs. At the end, three champions were left—one aged 12, one 15, and one 18.

grandparent of the games you may have played in video arcades or on your TV at home.

About ten years after the Brookhaven game was built, a scientist named Ralph Baer designed games that could be played on the video screen of a television set. Another scientist, Nolan Bushnell, created the first arcade video game. He used the profits from the game to start a company called Atari—now one of the world's largest producers of video games.

Today, you can play a variety of computerized games. Some, like STAR WARS and *Pac-Man*, test the quickness of a player's hands and eyes. Other computer games exercise your imagination by combining fantasy with problem solving. These interactive games—called that because the player and the computer react to one another during play—challenge you to figure out how to do such things as enter a castle across a moat full of crocodiles, play Sherlock Holmes and solve a complicated mystery, or fly and land an airplane.

Using a computer for (Continued on page 29)

Suiting up for a Photon game, Connie Horton, of Garland, Texas, puts on a helmet (above). Her friend Sheri Teer, of Mesquite, Texas, is already wearing hers. Next, they will enter a maze of fog-filled tunnels to play the futuristic game.

Gotcha! A Photon player zaps an opponent with a phaser—a pistol that shoots a light beam (left). A microprocessor inside the other player's control module—a pod connected to the helmet—records the hit and turns off that player's phaser for a few seconds. A central computer keeps track of all the action and totals the final score. "It felt like I was in a different world," says Sheri of her experience with Photon. "It's like playing cosmic cops," adds Connie.

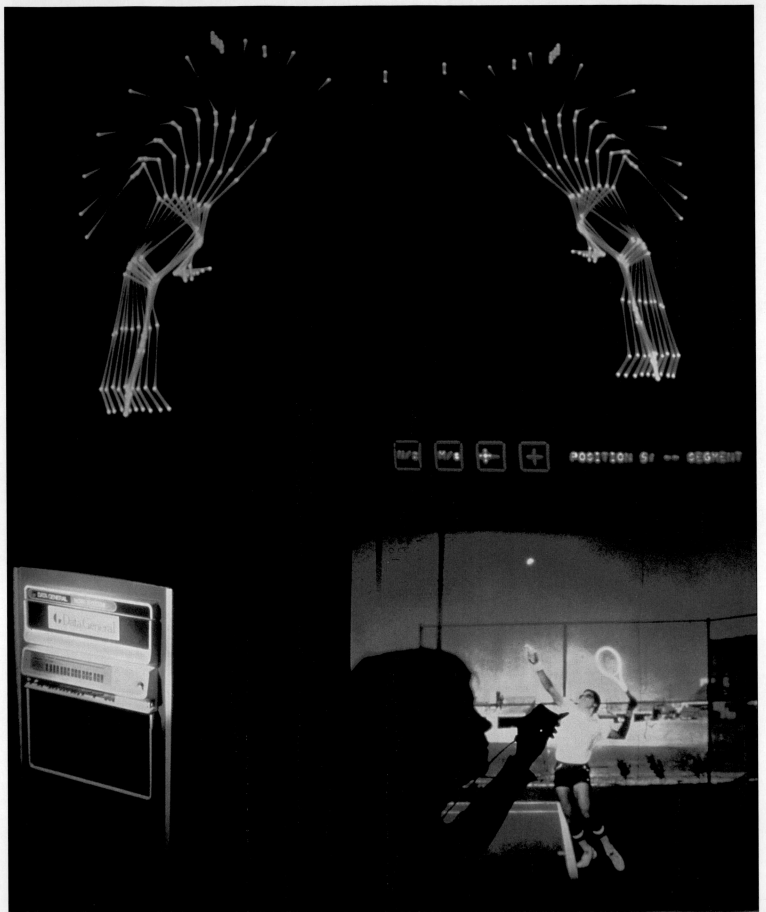

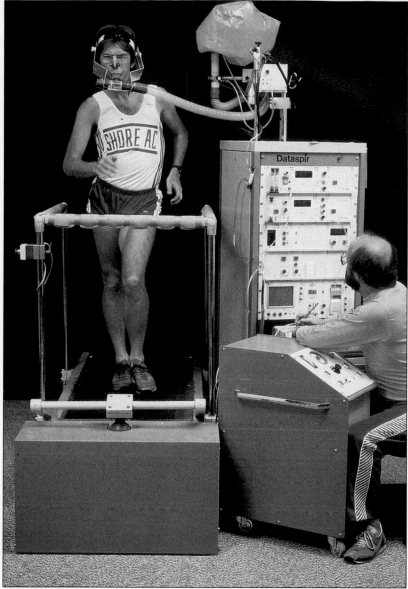

Olympic hopeful, racewalker Leonard Jansen takes a turn on a treadmill (above). As he walks, he breathes into equipment attached to a computer. The machine keeps track of how well Jansen's lungs are working. Dr. Peter Van Handel, a specialist in sports medicine, checks a printout of the results.

Stick figures play tennis on a screen (left). But this is no cartoon— it's a computer picture of a tennis player's body during a serve. Dr. Gideon Ariel, who developed the technique, uses a special pen to mark a film of the player. The computer converts the marks into stick figures that Dr. Ariel then slows down, studies, and analyzes. By studying his suggestions for improvement, tennis players and other athletes often can sharpen their sports skills.

(Continued from page 25) recreation often means playing games with your personal computer in the quiet of your own home. Another form of recreation— sports—also may involve computers. Nowadays, professional baseball players and coaches use computers to help record batting averages and other facts and figures. At big league games, coaches and players often share the dugout with a computer.

The world-class tennis player Martina Navratilova relies on computers to analyze her game. She also uses a computer to monitor her diet so that she eats the best possible foods to keep her body strong. The program, designed especially for the tennis champion by a diet expert, is called SMARTINA.

Many athletes make use of a computer technique developed by Dr. Gideon Ariel, a former Olympic discus thrower. Dr. Ariel's method allows athletes to see what they're doing in a completely new way—on a computer screen. Here's how it works. First, Dr. Ariel films the athlete in action. Then he plays back the film in slow motion. Every few frames, he stops the film and on it touches key areas of the athlete's body— such as elbows, knees, and other joints—with a special pen that feeds the positions of the touched areas to a computer. The computer then produces moving stick figures that show each tiny movement the athlete makes. By studying the stick figures, Dr. Ariel and the athletes work together to analyze movements, correct mistakes, and improve skills.

Athletes preparing for the 1984 Olympic games used such studies as they trained. Ariel's analysis helped make the United States women's volleyball team into one of the top three teams in the world. At the Olympic training center in Colorado Springs, Colorado, coaches used computers for many other training tasks as well. One system provided information on the strength of an athlete's lungs. Doctors could study the printouts from the system and suggest improvements in training routines.

When the well-trained U. S. athletes arrived in Los Angeles, California, for the games, they found themselves at the most computerized Olympics ever. Computers predicted the weather for Olympic sailors, and helped clothing organizers keep track of uniforms worn by the 60,000 officials and staff who crowded the games. Computers sent messages all around the sprawling city to keep officials and sports fans up to date on the results of the events.

Newspaper reporters covering the games used computerized word processors while writing their stories. Other computer programs provided them with background information about the various athletes they were watching. Nine hundred computer message boards announced information about schedule changes and upcoming events. Computers clocked race times and kept records of how the thousands of athletes participating in the games were doing. Computer graphic displays provided the audience at the Los Angeles Coliseum with close-up views of races and awards ceremonies. An artist even used a

Under an umbrella, scorekeepers use computers to enter results of the pole vault competition (above). The 1984 Olympic games in Los Angeles, California, were the most computerized ever.

As marathon runners enter the arena (right), two computer scoreboards show the crowd how they are doing. A computer clock below the Olympic torch shows exactly how many hours, minutes, and fractions of seconds the 26-mile (42-km) race has lasted.

At poolside, a staff member uses the electronic message system that linked Olympic events. People relied on 1,700 terminals like this one to keep track of competition at 23 different arenas.

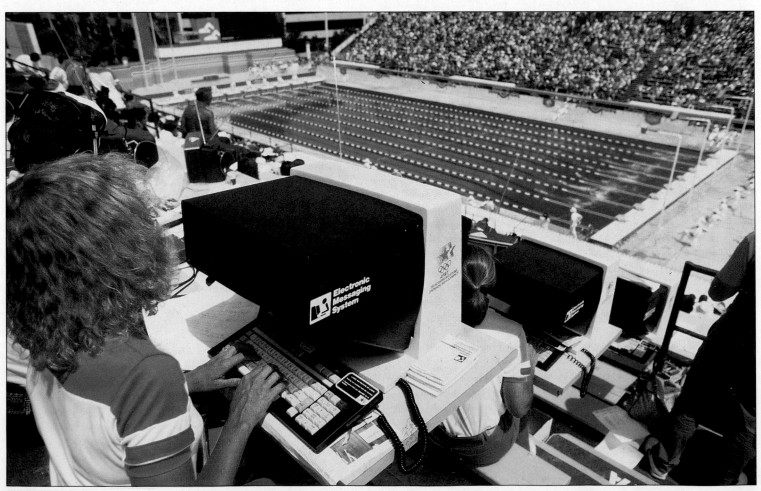

The scoreboard displays:

MARATHON MEN   WB 2:08.13
                 OB 2:09.55

49   596   GTIENO J.   KEN 2:24:13
50   789   LAFRANCHI   SUI 2:24:38
51   465   HOOPER D.   IRL 2:24:41
52   535   ADAMSON D.   JAM 2:25:02
53   728   CABAN C.   PUR 2:27:16
54   616   AGOSTA M.   LUX 2:27:41
55   80   THELFSN W.   RAT 2:29:21
56   160   SILVA A.   CHI 2:29:53

Clock: 2:35:56.2

GAMES of the XXIIIrd OLYMPIAD

LOS ANGELES CALIFORNIA 1984

computer to make colorful pictures of Olympic events.

Thousands of people enjoyed seeing huge images of talented athletes on the computerized displays in the Los Angeles Coliseum. Those images were presented on a screen made up of a grid of thousands of little dots called pixels. Pixel is a word that stands for "picture element." To make a computer image, a programmer types a string of numbers that assign each pixel a color and an intensity. The image appears on a screen when the computer processes all the numbers for all the pixels. Some pixels light up and others stay off. The combination of all the on and off lights adds up to a picture.

Physicist Melvin Prueitt uses a computer for his artistic creations—even though he claims he can't draw a straight line on his own. It's exciting to put numbers and other commands into a computer, and have a drawing like the butterfly below come out.

Computers enable artists to create images they could only dream of before. Here and on the next pages, you'll see what some imaginative computer artists have achieved, *(Continued on page 38)*

Computers can turn numbers into colorful images (right). Melvin Prueitt (below) creates pictures using a Cray supercomputer, one of the world's fastest and most powerful computers. He feeds the Cray detailed mathematical instructions about the shape, color, and location of the lines that will form his design. A physicist, Prueitt once used the Cray to design military weapons.

*B*irdlike characters Snoot and Muttly star in an animated movie produced entirely by computer (right). That's Snoot on the left.

To create a colorful eye (below), an artist converted a photograph into a computer image and changed the colors using a computer program.

A camera sensitive to the heat of infrared rays helped make a picture of a boy and his dog (bottom). The camera recorded the heat rays on magnetic tape. A computer then created an image showing different temperatures as different colors.

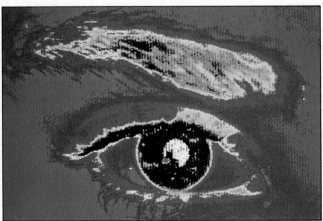

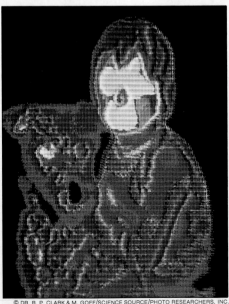

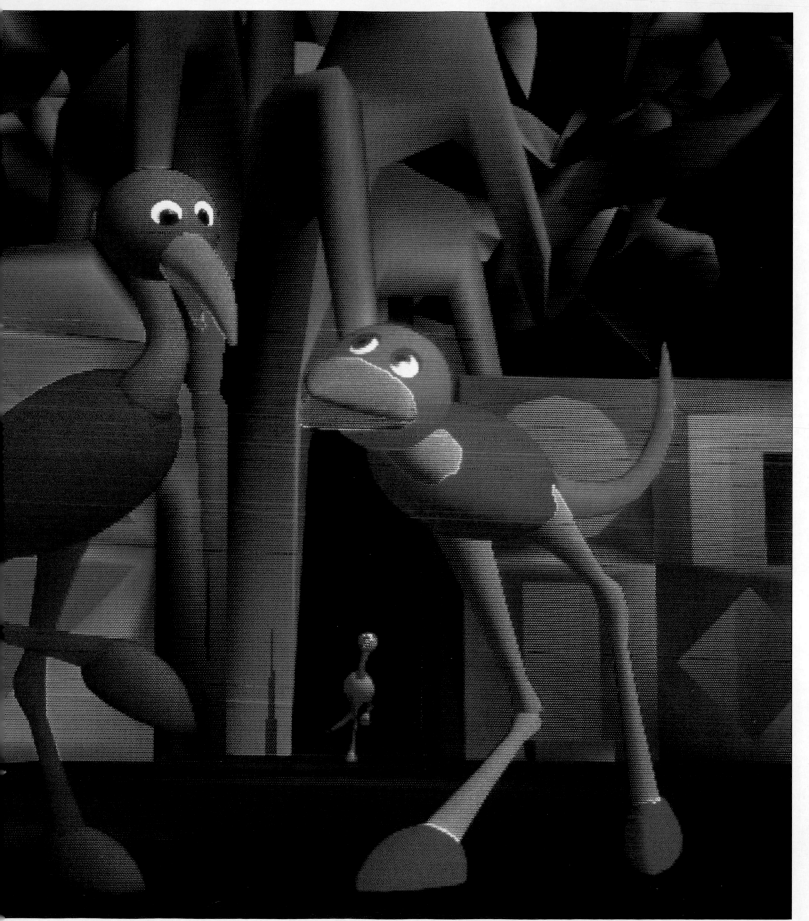

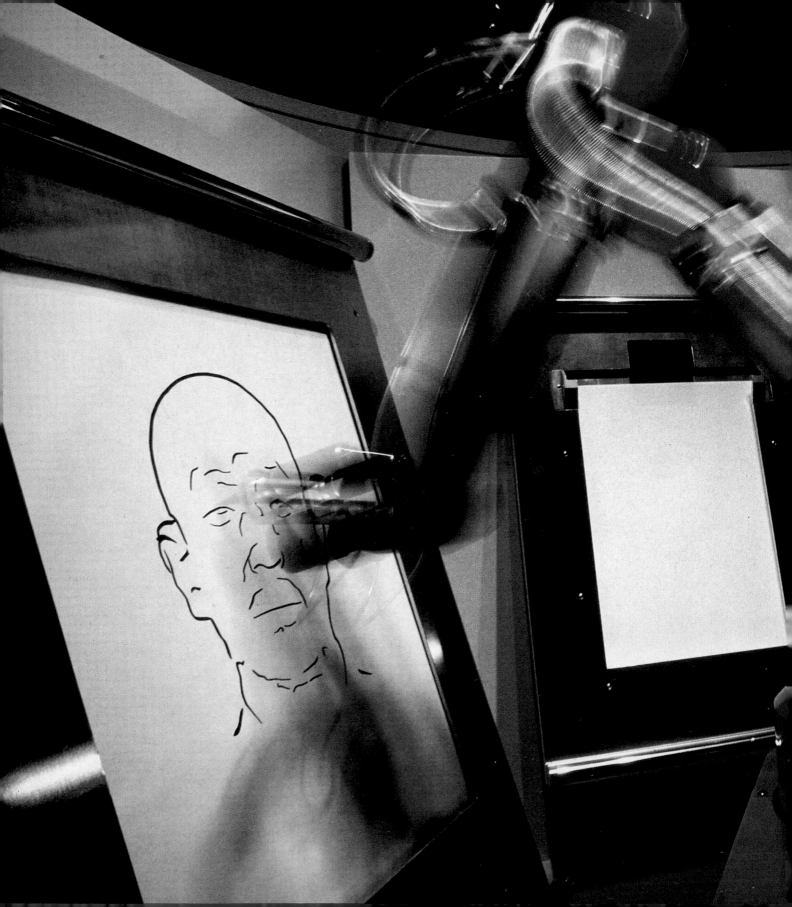

obot artist. At a Japanese science fair, a robotic arm attached to a camera sketches a portrait of a man. The camera scans the man's face for 20 seconds. Then the robotic hand draws lines representing the man's face and head. Although this robot entertains a lot of fairgoers, Japanese robotics engineers have more important plans for it. They hope it can lead the way to a future generation of super-robots that will be able to "see."

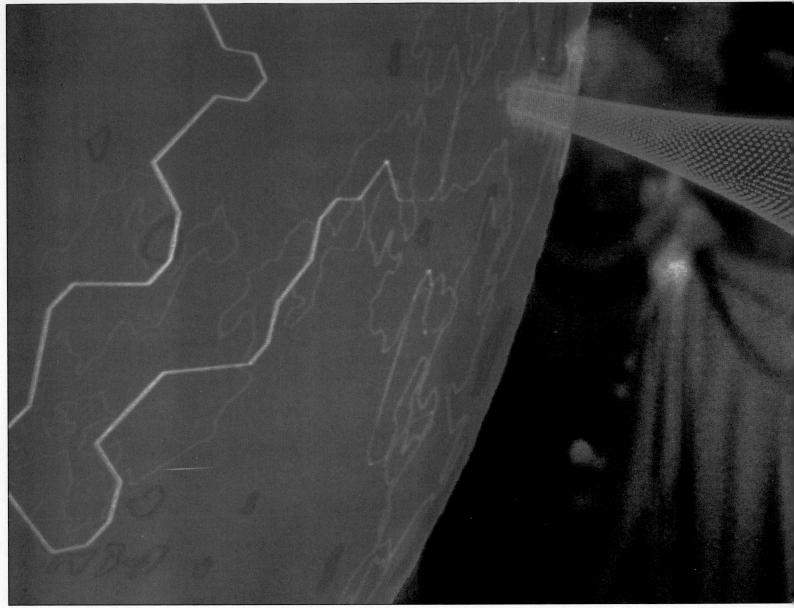

(Continued from page 32) using pixels instead of paint. It may take awhile for you to get used to the look of computerized art. You're probably familiar with computer effects used in movies, however. Today, more and more movies—from cartoons to space adventures—are produced with the help of computers.

Computers created many of the special effects in such movies as *Tron*, *Star Wars*, and *Star Trek II*. Without computers, many of the most thrilling scenes wouldn't have looked so exciting. Melvin Prueitt is one of the computer experts who is helping change the look of movies. Prueitt worked on computer art for three *Star Trek* movies.

At Lucasfilm, the company that produced *Star Wars*, moviemakers use computers to edit film, make sound tracks, and design graphics. Lucasfilm employs a staff of computer scientists who develop equipment to create new worlds on the screen. Pixar, one of the systems the team has invented, can draw eerie, outer-space backgrounds for use in the films.

If you saw *Star Wars*, you probably remember the robots that played such a large role in it. You may have wished that you could have a companion like C3PO or R2D2. For some people, having a robot companion around the house is already a reality. At places like Walt Disney's Magic Kingdom and Epcot

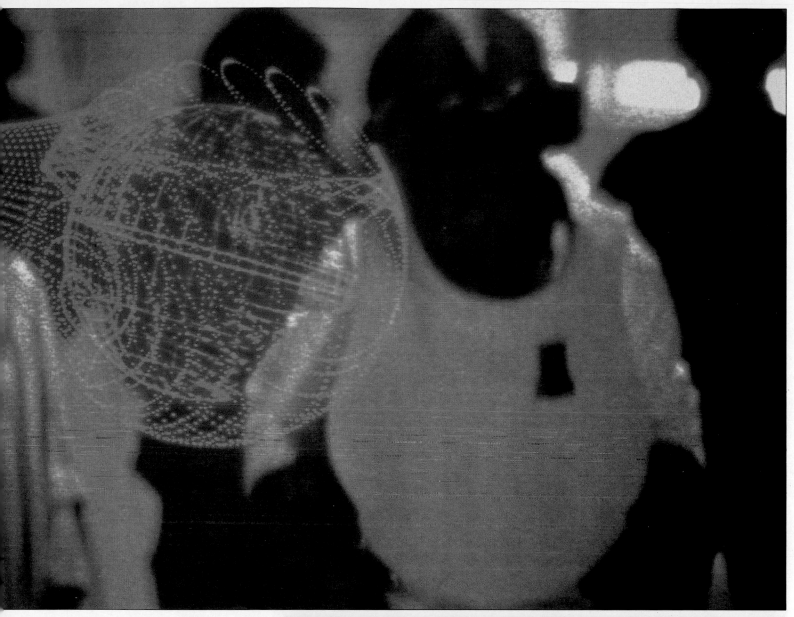

In the movie The Return of the Jedi, rebel forces study a moving, three-dimensional image as they plan an attack on the enemy "death star" (above). Computers helped create these special effects.

Lucasfilm engineers (right) may look relaxed, but they really work hard. For instance, the scene shown above took four months of computer programming and filming. The scene contains eight separate elements that were put together to make a single image of a planet and the death star.

39

That tickles! At Walt Disney World's Epcot Center, near Orlando, Florida, a technician adjusts the neck of a brontosaurus. The dinosaur munches grass, stretches its neck, and waves its jaw for guests visiting the Universe of Energy pavilion. What tells the model to move? Computers. Walt Disney World inventors call their computerized creations Audio-Animatronics figures.

In a lab, Disney engineers—known as "imagineers" at the company—program the movements of an Audio-Animatronics character (below). The figure is part of an old-time street scene at the World of Motion pavilion. A central computer system controls all the attractions at Epcot Center. It is programmed to make the voices, music, sound effects, and movement work together.

Center, near Orlando, Florida, robotlike figures are among the most popular entertainers.

The hundreds of Audio-Animatronics figures, as the people at Disney call them, take part in all kinds of attractions. There's a lively egg that sings and dances in one exhibit at Epcot Center. In another, figures of Benjamin Franklin and other historical characters move realistically. At yet another, Audio-Animatronics dinosaurs munch leaves and wave their heads at guests touring a prehistoric landscape.

All of the Disney Audio-Animatronics figures receive their instructions from a behind-the-scenes computer system. The system starts the music, controls the realistic movements the figures make, and starts their songs or speeches. The computers also stage-manage the timing of the show, from dimming the lights at its beginning to bringing down the curtain at its end.

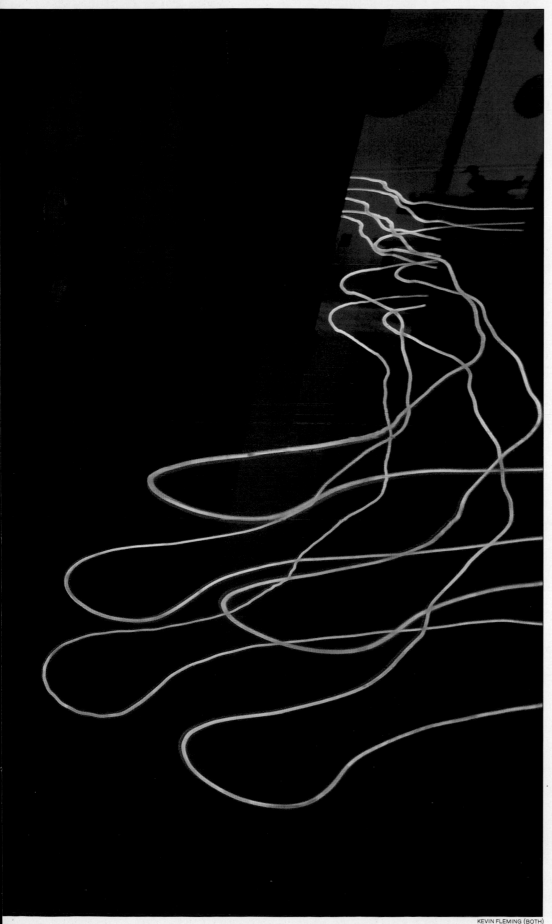

Never fear, Robart's here. Five small lights attached to a robot patrolling a house in Springfield, Virginia, show the winding path it follows as it does its job (left). The home-built robot, named Robart II, goes from room to room checking for fire and smoke, leaking gas, flooding, and intruders. If anything is wrong, Robart can sound a loud alarm or even turn on a sprinkler. A photographer used a time exposure to capture an image of Robart's trail of light. Below, Robart's inventor, Bart Everett, adjusts some of the electronic equipment—including nine microprocessors—that runs the robot. Everett is constantly improving his creation. He works with robots in his U. S. Navy job.

Computerized gardener. Jim Hill, of Covina, California, leans on his robot, Charlie (left). Hill is an amateur engineer, but the device he built is one of the most sophisticated home robots around. The 6-foot (2-m), 200-pound (91-kg) robot contains hundreds of computer chips and 30 motors. Charlie can even use a scanning light beam to "see" objects and figure out how far away they are.

Speak & Spell, a computerized toy (below), can recognize and speak hundreds of words when they are typed into it. But it recognizes only those words built into its circuits, shown beside it. A closed, one-purpose system like this is called a dedicated system.

Family input. The Barkers of Monterey, California, gather around their home computer as Amy, 7, uses it to make designs (below). Amy's brother Randall, 13, helped their father design the graphics program. They used BASIC, a simple programming language—once Randall had taught it to his dad.

MARK PERLSTEIN/BLACK STAR

ROGER RESSMEYER/STARLIGHT

He may not be as cute as C3PO, the robot in the movie *Star Wars*, but Charlie, the robot Jim Hill built from spare parts, makes a fine companion. Hill, who lives in Covina, California, is still improving his robot, which he built in his garage.

Microprocessors have brought the old dream of creating an all-purpose household robot closer to reality. Robots are simply machines. Some have computer brains. Robots can be very useful—but there are still problems with them. To be really efficient, robots need vision, a sense of touch, and the ability to respond to changes in their environment.

A typical robot used in industry today is much too dumb to help out around the house. Most industrial robots are just arms with tools attached to one end. Computers instruct the robots to do one job over and over again. In factories, robots do routine jobs such as spray-painting pieces of car bodies as they roll by. The robot does its job well, never complains, and takes no vacations. But it never knows when to stop. If

no car body part is rolling by, it simply sprays paint into the air. Most robots, unless instructed to do so, can't make decisions or change their actions.

In 1985, the U. S. Census Bureau—the people who count how many of us there are—began counting the American robot population. Even if the number is larger than expected, it won't be as large as the robot population in Japan. Some estimate that Japan has twice as many robots at work in its factories as the United States does. In the U. S., most robots work in the automobile industry.

Robotics, the science of developing robots, is booming in the U. S. as well as in Japan. Already several personal robots are available. They have names like Hero and Omnibot. They don't do much yet, but they can be a lot of fun. You can program them to do things like sing and dance, carry trays of snacks into your room, or pick the newspaper up off the porch. But that's about it. Perhaps by the 1990s, a robot as smart as C3PO may have become a reality.

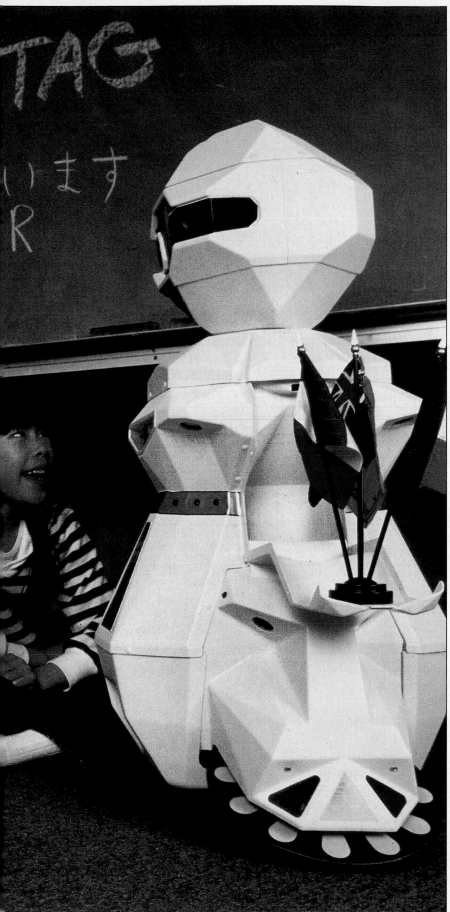

At Stevens Creek School, in Cupertino, California, elementary students learn three ways to say good morning to their "teacher," a Topo robot (left). Because the robot's voice synthesizer can create almost any sound, it can speak many languages, including German, Japanese, and French. Of course, Topo isn't a real teacher, but a teaching tool.

Rosalind Delgado, left, and Venice Clayton, both 13, share a keyboard in a computer class at Everett Middle School, in San Francisco (below). In the class, they learn to be comfortable with computers. At the same time, they improve their math and reading skills.

Someday you may run into a robot in a classroom—as the language students shown in the photograph on pages 46-47 did. You're even more likely to see—and to use—a computer in the classroom. In 1985, more than three-quarters of the public schools in the United States had classroom computers.

Schoolchildren in the Napa Valley, in California, don't have to go to their classroom to use computers; the classroom comes to them. An old school bus equipped with computer terminals rolls to many different schools in the district. Students in grades four through six climb aboard the Mobile Computer Lab to learn about programming. A school district in Idaho runs a similar computer bus.

Computer classes are so popular that unusual problems can result. In one school, in New Orleans, Louisiana, teachers had trouble getting some of the students who were using the newly installed computers to go home at the end of the school day.

Many teachers think that computers play a valuable role in education. For one thing, the machines make good tutors. They're patient, even when a student repeats an exercise many times. They also correct work immediately—something you'll appreciate if you've ever spent a week waiting for your teacher to return a spelling test.

Computers give a learner individual attention during math and grammar drills. And they allow the learner to proceed at any pace—either faster or slower than the class average.

Computer education can be even more useful, some educators believe, when students actually

---

On the road. A star-spangled bus containing a computer classroom rolls through the countryside near Napa, California (below). To add to the limited number of computers in the Napa school system, 21 schools in the area share the bus, called the Mobile Computer Lab. It has enough computers for 16 students and a teacher. At right, fifth and sixth graders from Carneros School sit at work stations inside the lab. One student receives advice from a teacher about a graphics program he wrote himself, using a programming language called PILOT. This language can be used to create both images and sounds.

Breakdance! Colorful computer images demonstrate arm positions for a dance routine (right). Below each image, Miles Efron, 13, of Palo Alto, California, turns the pictures into action. The computer figure's arms can be moved to different positions as programmers invent routines. Then the pictures can be run together in a moving cartoon.

With the help of Jillian Dorman, whose company prepared the program, dance students watch a dance routine they'll perform (below). During the summer that Torkwase Mshuja, 10, at right, and Anne Marie Hiskes, 10, of Palo Alto, took part in the class, breakdancing was popular. But not many dancers used a computer to perfect their skills.

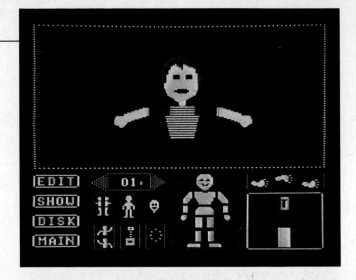

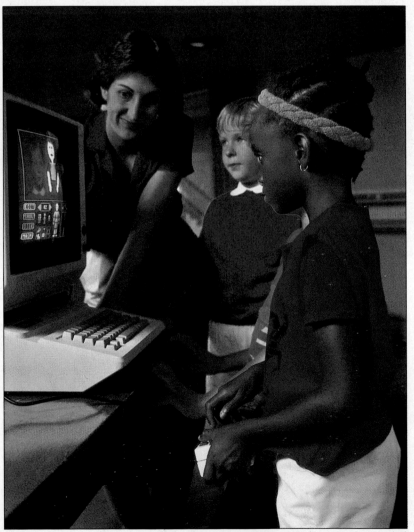

learn to write programs for the computer. To write a program, you have to organize your thinking and plan your program in a precise, step-by-step way. Suppose you wanted to program a computer to peel an orange. You'd have to figure out exactly how many steps are involved in that action, and explain each one clearly. That's more complicated than it sounds. Dividing a task into its different parts helps computer students think logically—an important part of the learning process.

Sometimes, computers take the place of teachers entirely. At Stanford, a large university in California, students can sign up for a course in logic. The class is taught entirely by computer. No professor ever stands before the class.

The logic course involves 29 lessons, all of them at a computer terminal. Students do the work at their own pace. Some spend 30 hours taking the course; others use more than 100 hours. The computer gives

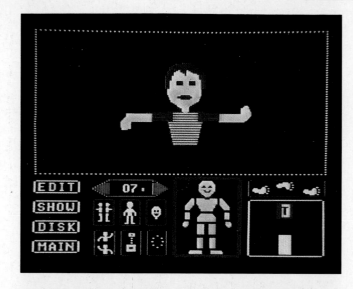

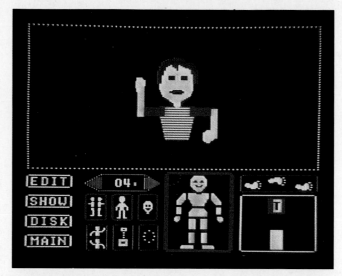

helpful hints, figures out grades—and even accepts criticism from its students. Part of the logic computer program allows learners to type in their gripes about the course.

Another kind of computer learning goes on at Stanford University. Students at Stanford's Children's Dance Workshop use a computer to create their own dances—including breakdances.

Elizabeth Larkam, a dancer, runs the workshop. She chose breakdancing because she knew it was popular with students. "I knew children would respond well," she says. "I wanted to attract older children, ages 8 to 12, who already had some computer exposure."

Ms. Larkam worked with a computer programmer to design the software used in the dance workshop. They came up with a program that uses movable stick figures. Users choose body and arm positions from a menu, or listing, of items. Then they can watch the figures perform the dance they have designed.

Computer users can choose from hundreds of different educational software programs. Designing software is big business. In 1983, buyers spent 450 million dollars on educational software. Half of those buyers were families purchasing the programs to use on home computers.

Recently, educational software and hardware makers decided to test their products on some of the toughest judges around—the children who use them. In 1984, at the Disneyland Convention Center, in Anaheim, California, more than 50 companies exhibited their new products at an exhibit called *Bits & Bytes,* the first interactive computer show for children.

"The computer industry can learn from seeing its products tested under 'battlefield' conditions," says a staff member of the *Bits & Bytes* show. The battlefield was crowded: Fifteen thousand people came to the convention center to try out the latest programs, from

Computer enthusiasts crowd the Bits & Bytes show, in Anaheim, California (right). Called "the first interactive computer show for kids," Bits & Bytes attracted about 15,000 people. They saw and tried the latest computer products for home and school. Here, boys and girls test new programs. More than 50 computer companies displayed their latest products.

"Pleased to meet you, Specky." Mary Lee Lindsey, 5, and her sister Monica, 7, of El Monte, California, get acquainted with a robot (below) at the Bits & Bytes show. "Specky moved around and talked to all the children," says Monica. The robot spoke both English and Spanish.

speedreading drills to fantasy invention games.

The Lindseys, a family from El Monte, California, arrived at ten o'clock in the morning, planning to make a quick tour of the show. Ten hours later they were still there. "We had a great time at the show," Mr. Lindsey reported. During the day, they met Specky the Robot, who moved around the convention center chatting with visitors. Mary Lee Lindsey, 5, especially enjoyed Specky. "He talks funny, and he's my size," Mary Lee said.

The *Bits & Bytes* organizers plan to put on several similar shows, each in a different city in the United States. Will the shows become boring? They don't think so. Things change so fast in the computer industry that *Bits & Bytes* organizers look forward to having a lot of new material to show off each year.

It's hard to imagine, but computers haven't really been around that long. Scientists only recently developed the equipment that allows computers to accomplish the many useful and entertaining things they do in our lives. In the next chapter, you'll find out more about the scientific technology that makes computers the amazing machines they are today.

Jamie Bussey, 10, of Modesto, California, right, introduces 9-year-old Steven Bates, of Santa Ana, to a program called JUST IMAGINE (below). "It's a program where you can create a story using graphics and animation," says Jamie. He had a job demonstrating Commodore computer products to teachers and students who visited the show.

FROM SAND TO SILICON

Whether wall-size or wrist-size, computers handle a lot of information quickly. The units along the wall, called tape drives, store records for the National Geographic Society's central computer. The two microcomputers in the foreground could be used to balance a checkbook or to write a book report. Alexandra Fastov, 10, of Washington, D. C., wears a watch that doubles as a calculator.

DECLAN HAUN

55

Have you ever thought about what the word "compute" means? Look it up in the dictionary and you'll discover that one definition is "to make calculations." In other words, to compute means to figure things out using mathematics. Computing can be as simple as adding 2 + 2. It can also be complex, as it is when NASA scientists compute a space shuttle's course.

People have been computing ever since they started counting on their fingers. If you've ever used that method to do your math, you know it's not very efficient. That's why people have invented systems of all kinds to help them solve mathematical problems. Early record keepers probably kept track of small numbers by laying pebbles on the sand. The people of China have relied on a device called an abacus (AB-uh-cuss)—a frame containing beads strung on wires—for thousands of years. Many people still use the abacus to add, subtract, multiply, and divide.

Before electricity was used to power machines, scientists struggled to build mechanical equipment to help them make calculations. A British mathematician named Charles Babbage devoted much of his life to developing ideas for such machines. Unfortunately, he never built a machine that worked. Tools for making the parts necessary for Babbage's machine hadn't been invented yet. Even if Babbage had built a successful mechanical calculator, it would have been complicated and difficult to operate.

For a machine to do complex mathematical calculations quickly and accurately, it needs electronic and magnetic parts. Such parts can store information and send it from one part of the machine to another. By the mid-20th century, engineers had developed such technology. Machines finally were built that could

take data, work with it, and come up with answers by controlling the flow of electricity through their circuits. The first of these machines went into action in the mid-1940s. It was called ENIAC, and it weighed 30 tons (27 t). Its circuits worked using vacuum tubes. ENIAC was hot and slow, and it used a huge amount of power—but it could add 5,000 ten-digit numbers a second. The first generation of computers was born.

In 1947, scientists at Bell Telephone Laboratories, in New Jersey, came up with a new device called a transistor. A transistor acts as a tiny switch that can be turned on and off quickly with small amounts of electric current. Transistors enabled engineers to build computers that were smaller, ran on less power, and solved problems ten times faster than the first generation of computers.

About ten years later, two electronics engineers

Back in the 1820s, an English scientist named Charles Babbage had an idea. He designed a machine to compute mathematical problems and print the answers. The design for his "Difference Engine" looked like this model (right). Although he worked on his invention for years, Babbage couldn't get machine parts exact enough to make the device work. But he had the right idea—as the modern computer later proved.

independently came up with an even better—and smaller—piece of equipment than the transistor. It was the integrated circuit, or IC. Circuits are the electronic connections along which electricity and coded information move inside a computer. Circuits make it possible for the machine to do its job. An integrated circuit combines many components—parts—on a single piece of material called silicon. ICs, usually called chips, were much smaller and faster than transistors. They led to the third generation of computers.

Soon, engineers figured out how to pack a number of circuits onto the small chips. Today, chips the size of a baby's fingernail contain thousands of circuits. These little chips—known as microprocessors—are powerful enough to do the same kinds of calculations that the huge ENIAC did—and do them hundreds of times faster. Microprocessors *(Continued on page 60)*

Ultramodern and superpowerful, the CRAY X-MP computer can do a billion computations a second. The illustration below combines a photograph of the CRAY X-MP system with a computer graphic. Computer scientists use Cray computers for complex jobs such as forecasting weather and designing automobiles and aircraft. Other experts use Cray computers to produce special effects like those in such movies as The Last Starfighter.

57

*W*hat happens after you push the keys on a computer and the machine starts working? Pretend that the computer is a factory. In factories, raw material is changed into new products that people can use. The drawing on the right shows how a computer "factory" processes its raw material—information. A girl sits at an INPUT device, a keyboard much like that of a typewriter. She types a program to solve the arithmetic problem (2 + 3 = ?). A chip in the computer translates the numbers and letters on the keys she strikes into a language the computer can use easily—electrical pulses. These pulses travel to the CENTRAL PROCESSING UNIT, or CPU—the supervisor and timekeeper of the factory. At incredibly high speed, the CPU tells the other parts of the computer how to process the data and when to do it. The CPU sends the problem to the MEMORY. The memory is like a huge library of instruction manuals containing directions for how to do things. The CPU pulls together instructions on problem solving that are stored in various parts of the memory. Then it sends the instructions to the ARITHMETIC LOGIC UNIT, or ALU—a kind of assembly area. The ALU makes any decisions or calculations needed and sends the result wherever the CPU instructs it to. Now it's time for the finished product—the answer to the problem—to show up on the OUTPUT devices. One of these, the MONITOR, or screen, displays the answer. If the boy wants a printed copy of the problem and answer, a command typed to the CPU can order the PRINTER, another output device, to print it on a piece of paper.

(Continued from page 57) are often called "computers on a chip." They brought about the fourth, and latest, generation of computers.

Progress in the computer industry has taken place rapidly. In only 40 years, computers have advanced from huge, slow, expensive machines to the quick, powerful, and affordable ones so many people use today. Chips run an amazing variety of computers, from the little calculator you may have on your wristwatch to the CRAY X-MP, a supercomputer that can solve a billion mathematical problems in one second.

Although a computer can't match your brain for figuring most things out, even a small computer can do math calculations much more quickly than you can. It does them in somewhat the same way. Let's say someone asks you to add two numbers together. You hear the problem with your ears or see it with your eyes. Your eyes or ears are acting as input devices to pass the problem along to your brain. On a computer, the input device is probably a keyboard.

Once the problem reaches your brain, you call on your memory to help solve it. You recall how to add, something you learned back when you were in first grade. To work out the answer, you process the information you took in through your eyes or ears, using the method you called up from your memory. A computer does much the same thing. An arithmetic chip is programmed to add. Circuits move the numbers from the keyboard, through the CPU—the computer's brain—to the arithmetic unit.

Once you've figured out the answer, you either say it or write it down. Your voice or your pencil and paper are your output devices. The computer's output devices are a screen, which shows the answer in lit-up characters, or a printer, which prints the answer on paper.

As you're thinking about how to come up with the right answer to the problem, you're using language. You may think, "Let's see, 9 + 7 = 16." Inside the computer, however, the numbers tapped into the machine change into a different kind of language.

When you type a letter, a number, or a symbol such as a "+" on a computer keyboard, you begin a process that will be carried out by pulses of electricity. The computer uses a series of on-and-off pulses to keep track of the information it's processing and what it's supposed to do with the data, or processed information. The pulses aren't random, of course. They're

JOHN F. PORTER (ART)

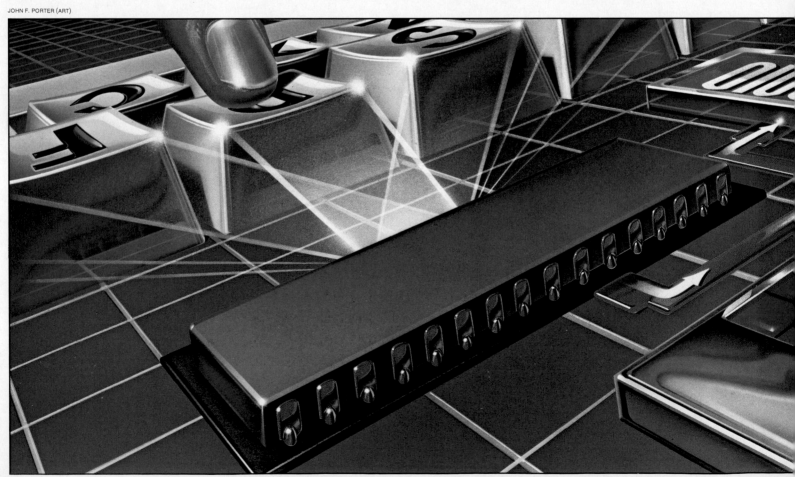

arranged in a carefully worked out system called the binary code. "Binary" means that the code has two parts. One part, the number 1, stands for "on," or the presence of an electrical pulse. The other part, a zero, stands for "off," or the absence of a pulse. Morse Code is a binary code. It uses dots and dashes or short and long pulses instead of on-and-off pulses. The on-and-off pulses of a computer's binary code are created—and move—incredibly fast.

A common computer binary code is the American Standard Code for Information Interchange, or ASCII. It uses series of its two digits to stand for letters, numbers, and symbols. If your name starts with A, for example, the A looks like this in ASCII: 01000001. In electronic pulses, that's *off, on, off, off, off, off, off, on.* Every time you tap a capital A on a computer keyboard, the chips inside the computer translate the letter into that particular group of pulses. A single on or off pulse is called a bit, a computer word that stands for "binary digit." Each letter of the alphabet and each number has its own series of ons and offs in binary code. The ASCII code travels through a computer's circuits in groups of eight bits like the one you've just seen. These eight-part groups are called bytes.

Now watch what happens when you hit the letter D on a computer keyboard (1). The drawing below shows how a tiny electronic device called a chip (2) registers the keystroke. The chip, which constantly scans the keyboard, changes the letter into a series of on-and-off pulses of electricity that stand for D. The pulses move to the CPU (3). The CPU translates this series of pulses into a computer code called ASCII. The CPU then consults the program in memory to find out what to do with the code—in this case, display it on the screen. The code moves on to a chip called a character generator (4). It turns on and off the right number of pixels—spots of light—on the screen (5) to form the letter D in WORLD.

Tiny electronic switches on the chips inside a computer create the binary code. The switches turn the current on and off. While the computer is operating, thousands—and in some computers hundreds of billions—of these switches are at work every second. Like trains on tracks, the pulses move along circuits. They pass through switches called gates, arranged in patterns. A chip may have thousands of gates on it. The gates change the pattern of pulses on their trip through the machine, enabling the computer to do a variety of tasks.

It's hard to believe that all this can be carried out by devices as small as chips are. But the microchip is a powerful tool—so powerful that it may surprise you to learn that the silicon it's made from comes from a very common substance: quartz rock.

Chip manufacturers melt and purify the quartz and use it to make long silicon crystals. These are sliced into thin wafers. A chip designer creates a blueprint of circuit patterns called the chip's architecture. These patterns are reduced and then carved into the silicon by a series of chemical processes.

Finally, the chips are inspected, tested, and enclosed in protective cases. They're sent off to become a brain, a memory, or some other part of a computer. The chips will do some remarkable things. In the next chapter, you'll find out what they are doing for some of the people who work in science and industry.

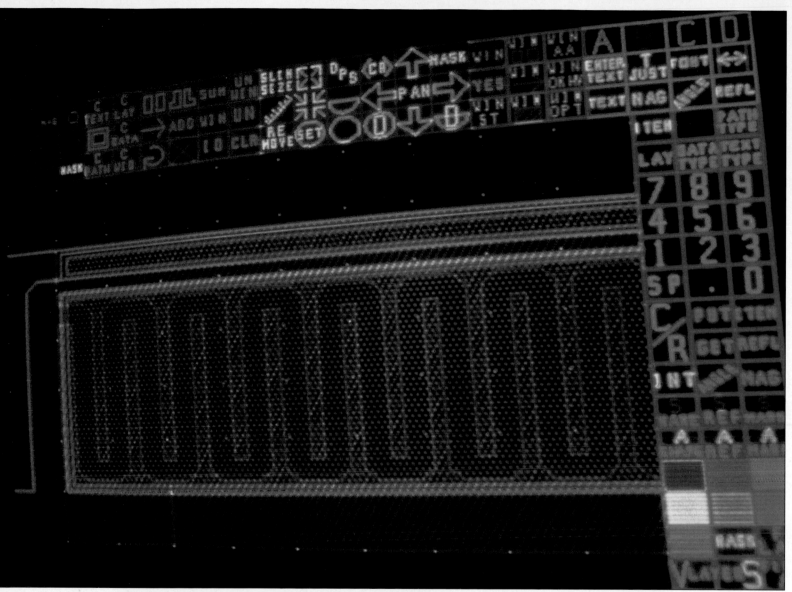

Computing a chip. At Atari, an engineer works on a circuit design for a chip (above). The computer he uses allows him to try out different ways of connecting the circuits. A black hood over the computer monitor makes it easier to see the design on the screen.

Already packaged, a chip looks small compared with even a tiny part of its design (left). During the chip-making process, the design was reduced photographically to fit on the silicon slice that forms the chip.

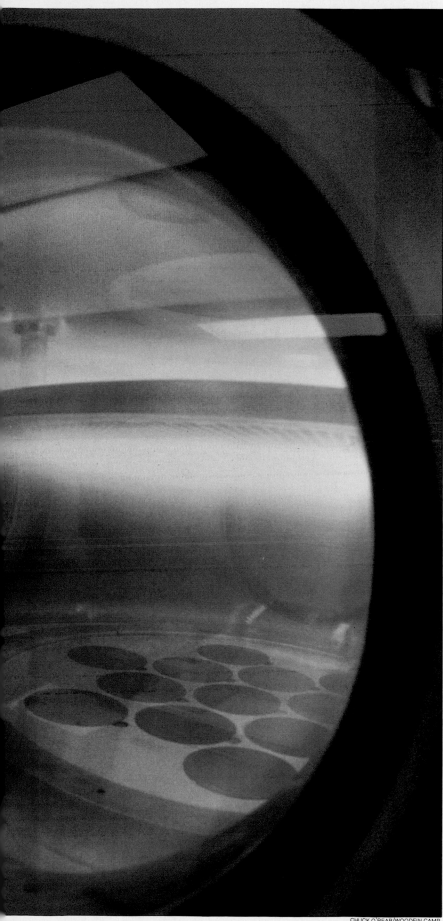

Something's in the oven. It's computer chips, not chocolate chip cookies. At IBM, an engineer adjusts a vacuum chamber holding silicon wafers (left). Engineers have used a special photographic process to print a pattern of circuits on each wafer. Inside the chamber, superhot gases will eat away surface areas not covered with circuits. The wafers will be cut into chips that will run computers.

Wafer inspector. Dressed in clothing designed to keep dirt particles from escaping into the air, an operator at Linear Technology Corporation checks a silicon wafer for particles (below). Even a tiny speck of dust can ruin the delicate workings of a computer chip. Chips must be manufactured in "clean rooms" in which the air is as pure as possible. Chip-making facilities are up to 1,000 times cleaner than hospital operating rooms.

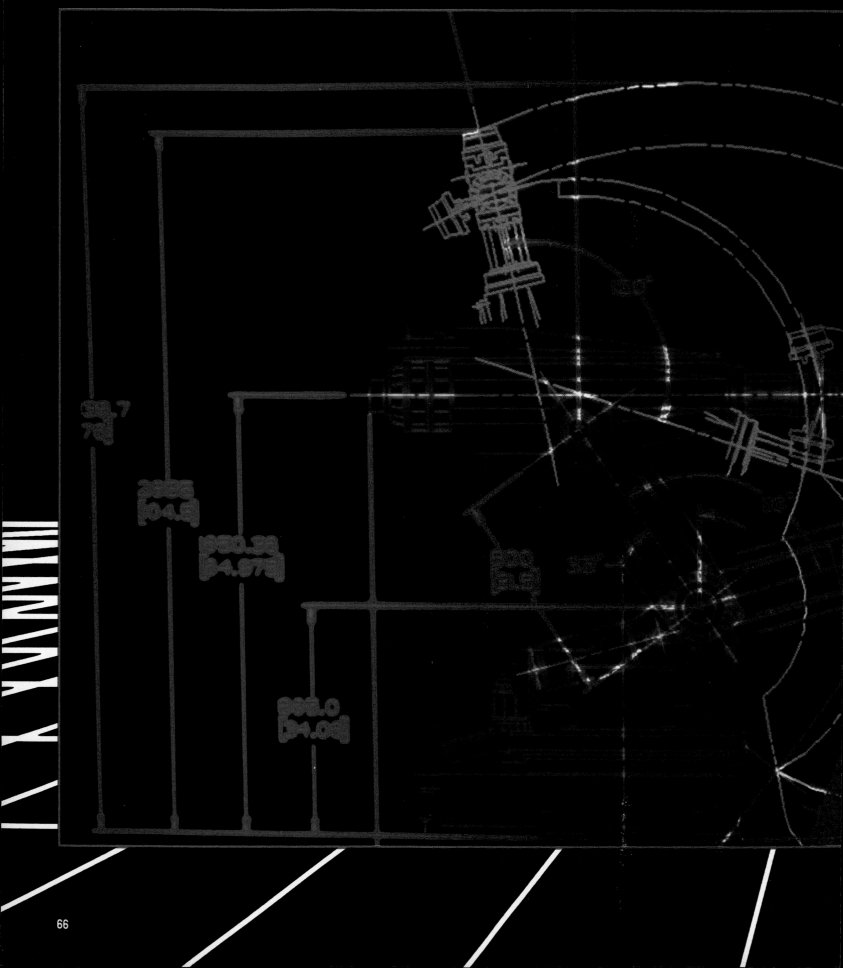

NEW TOOLS FOR THE WORKPLACE

Computer-aided design, or CAD, helps engineers invent new machines. At left, a CAD drawing produced on a computer screen shows a model robotic arm. In industry, an arm like this will put liners into refrigerators and lift heavy parts and materials in a production line. In the picture, the arm isn't doing anything. The lines show the movements that an arm will make when it's in action.

DAN McCOY/RAINBOW

Have you ever wondered how engineers come up with a design for a jet plane or a new car? These days, a computer probably had something to do with it.

Computers play important roles in many industries, from car manufacturing to cosmetics. People use computers for a lot of different jobs, from keeping track of the money a business earns to sending out bills and writing letters. At companies around the world, engineers and designers have added computers, terminals, and light pens to the tools of their trade. Light pens are devices that enter or change data when touched to a computer screen. The process they use is called CAD—computer-aided design.

CAD is used in designing improved wings for airplanes and better hatchbacks for cars. The methods that work well for large pieces of complicated equipment can be applied to other products, too. A silverware manufacturer, for example, uses CAD to design knives, forks, and spoons. CAD has improved the design of fire hydrants and running shoes, as well as that of oil rigs and space equipment. Some toy makers use CAD. McDonald's plans to use French-fry cookers redesigned by CAD. Engineers even use CAD to come up with new computer chips.

Computers save designers a lot of time. Instead of having to redo blueprints each time they make a tiny change, designers simply push a few buttons on a keyboard, and a new version of the design appears on a screen. Then a printer provides them with paper copies of the finished version.

CAD programs let designers do more than just make their drawings better. The programs also enable computers to test how well different kinds of

Model airplane with a difference. Michelle Haffner, a computer programmer with the Boeing Company, checks out a model of a plane called a 767 (below). She helped design the CAD program that engineers used when they designed the 767. The grid of lines on the model is called a wire-frame drawing. It was produced by a computer.

products will perform—without actually manufacturing them. This process is called simulation.

Simulating something is pretending that it's really happening. Let's say you're designing an airplane, and you want to find out how well its different parts would work during flight. One way to do that would be to build the plane and take off. That method would work—but it could be expensive and dangerous. You might discover that, at 300 miles an hour (483 km/h), the plane would begin to fall apart.

Computer simulations allow engineers to draw a plane, and then test it to see whether its structure would stand up under the stresses of flight. The plane never leaves the screen of the computer terminal. If the experiment shows that the design has weaknesses, it's back to the drawing board—or to the terminal.

Computer simulations can be used to solve many kinds of "what if" problems. With CAD to help, products can be designed for everyone to use. Not all the "what if" questions have to do with safety or convenience, however.

Sometimes people in industry use computers to help them make things look more attractive. That's what the program called AUTOCOLOR, now being tested at General Motors Research Laboratories, in Warren, Michigan, does. It answers the questions "What if light hit this car from above? Would it look better bouncing off a metallic gray car or a bright red one?"

Some automotive companies use a software package called SAMMIE when they design cars. SAMMIE appears as a figure on a *(Continued on page 72)*

Experimental computer programs help experts at the General Motors Research Laboratories plan tomorrow's cars (below). One program, called AUTOCOLOR, shows how different paint colors reflect light. It enables designers to find the most pleasing shades. The three line drawings show light hitting a model car from different angles. At upper right, another program calculates how a stream of air would affect an experimental model.

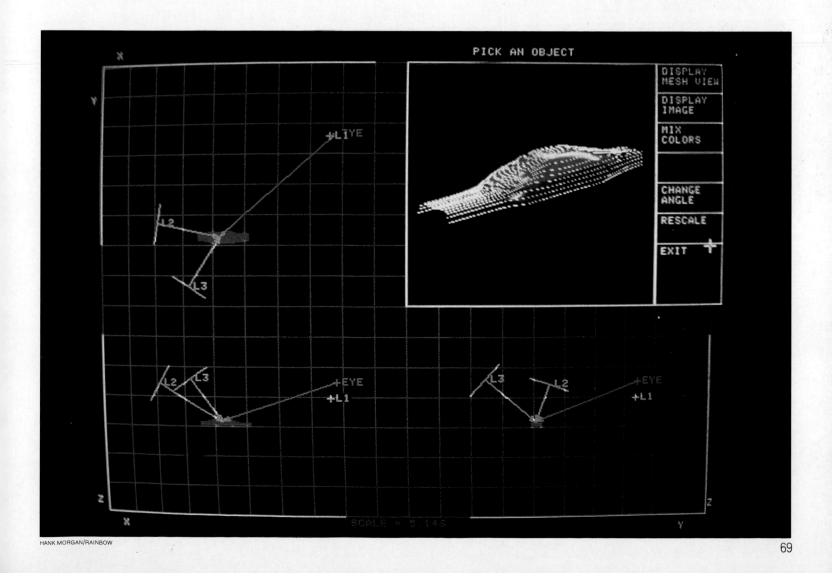

Sparks fly as car bodies move along an assembly line in a Chrysler factory (right). The workers doing the welding won't get burned, however. They're robots. Chrysler first put robotic welders in one of its factories in 1977. Welding like this must be done just right every time. The robots are good at it—and they don't get bored. Chrysler offered programs that helped the people who once did this work learn other jobs.

Making a delivery, a computer-controlled vehicle called Prontow glides down an aisle at a Burlington Industries factory (below). Prontow drops off yarn for weaving and delivers finished fabric to the shipping area. On its trips through the factory, the machine follows wires set into grooves in the floor.

(Continued from page 69) computer screen and simulates the actions of a human. SAMMIE can be programmed to be short or tall. That lets a car designer see if the way a steering wheel fits into a dashboard would be as comfortable for someone more than 6 feet (2 m) tall as it would be for someone much shorter. SAMMIE also tests reach, movement, and vision.

Computers not only help engineers and designers complete and test a car's design, but they also play a large role in the manufacture of the cars themselves. Computer-controlled robots weld body parts together, apply paint, and perform several other tasks. Computers turn up *inside* cars, too.

If your family owns a new car, you're probably familiar with some computerized features. Does your car talk to you, reminding you that the keys are in the ignition or that the door is open? That's a synthesized computer voice you're hearing. Is there a digital

Sushi chef. It takes a human being to add the raw fish, but a robot forms the rice cakes used in making sushi, a favorite Japanese food (below). Controlled by a microchip, the robot can form enough rice cakes in an hour to feed 150 people—that's about 1,200 pieces. The machine has been in use in Japan for several years. Recently, restaurants in the United States have begun installing similar sushi machines.

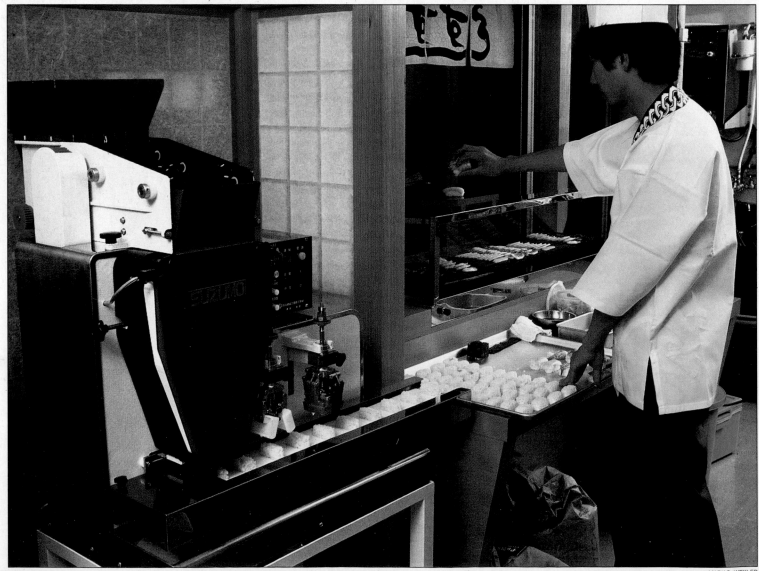

display in the dashboard that tells you how many miles you've traveled and how many you still have to go? A computer does the arithmetic to display those numbers. Meanwhile, under the hood, another computer keeps track of how well the engine is performing, and makes adjustments as the car runs.

Even though you may be familiar with computers in cars, would you expect to find one in a restaurant? In many Japanese restaurants, a robot presses rice into the small cakes that are one ingredient of sushi, a raw-fish dish. The robot presses rice cakes three times faster than a human chef can. The robot hasn't been programmed for the delicate job of adding the fish to the rice, however. The chef and the robot work together to produce the finished dish.

Many people are teaming up with computers to make their jobs easier—and more interesting. One unusual computer program has found its way into the cosmetics section of department stores. ELIZABETH, a program used by makeup specialists at Elizabeth Arden, Inc., answers "what if" questions about makeup. On a screen, the computer simulates three different makeup looks for a customer's face. A printout reminds the customer how to achieve the effects. Another kind of machine, called a "skin imaging computer," analyzes a customer's skin type and suggests ways to care for it. For this device, beauty experts use technology similar to that used by the National Aeronautics and Space Administration's moon-mapping computers.

Of course, buying a brand-new computerized car, eating sushi in a Japanese restaurant, or seeing a cosmetic consultant all cost money. So where do people get the cash? Most head for a bank—where they withdraw their money by computer.

A piggy bank can be a good place to keep small

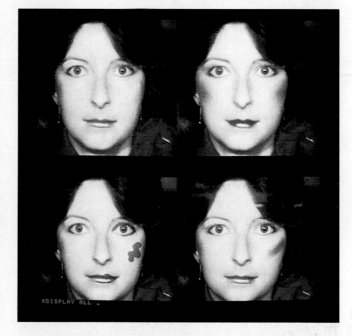

ELIZABETH, a computer make-over system developed by the Elizabeth Arden company, helps a model try on makeup—without the makeup. When beauty expert Jerry Hamilton-Catty (left) touched the pressure-sensitive tabletop with the stylus he's holding, makeup colors appeared on the TV screen. He selected the shade on a control board. The pictures above—counterclockwise from upper left—show each step he took in applying the blush, or cheek color.

amounts of money, but if you have saved more than a few dollars, you may decide to keep it in an account at a bank. And your bank probably keeps track of your money with a computer.

Many banks provide customers with computer-coded cards that enable them to communicate with automatic teller machines. At any time of the day or night, people who use these cards can withdraw cash from their accounts, add money to them, or ask the computer how much money they have remaining in the account.

The United States government does much of its banking by computer. The Federal Reserve System, the nation's central bank, uses a computer system called Fedwire to transfer money among its thousands of member banks. Every day, billions of dollars move from bank to bank. No paper or coins change hands. Using Fedwire, bankers subtract money from one account and add it to another somewhere else. Each transaction takes only a few minutes.

Citicorp, a large international bank, is experimenting with a new kind of computer system. Some of the bank's customers are trying out a computer terminal about the size of a large hand-held calculator. Using it, the customers can sit at home while they balance their checkbooks or transfer their money from one account to another. Soon they may even use it to pay certain bills.

At a hospital in Boston, Massachusetts, specialists examine an elderly "patient" named Ankh-pef-hor. He's more than 2,000 years old. Using a method called computerized tomography, or CT, experts get a close look at the ancient Egyptian—without disturbing the mummy's rare gilded (Continued on page 79)

Moving a million? It's hard work to transfer funds, as Erin Screen, 8, of Annandale, Virginia, and Sam Adkins, 10, of Washington, D. C., found out (left). To move a million dollars in small bills, they'd have to make a lot of trips with their wagon. Of course, banks don't move money that way. Bank employees transfer funds quickly and safely by computer—as the woman at the terminal demonstrates.

Computing cattle. On their Missouri farm, members of the Beckett family use a personal computer to keep track of their herd (right). Melesa Beckett enters facts about the animal being inspected by, from the left, Bill Miller; her husband, John; and Bill's father, Gene. The Becketts also receive the latest farm news from a data base.

Farmer's helper. Bob Johnson carries his computer through his farmyard on a wintry day (below). He uses it in running the Illinois farm where he and his family raise soybeans, corn, and hogs. He also uses a computer-controlled sprayer on his tractor when he treats his crops with pest killer.

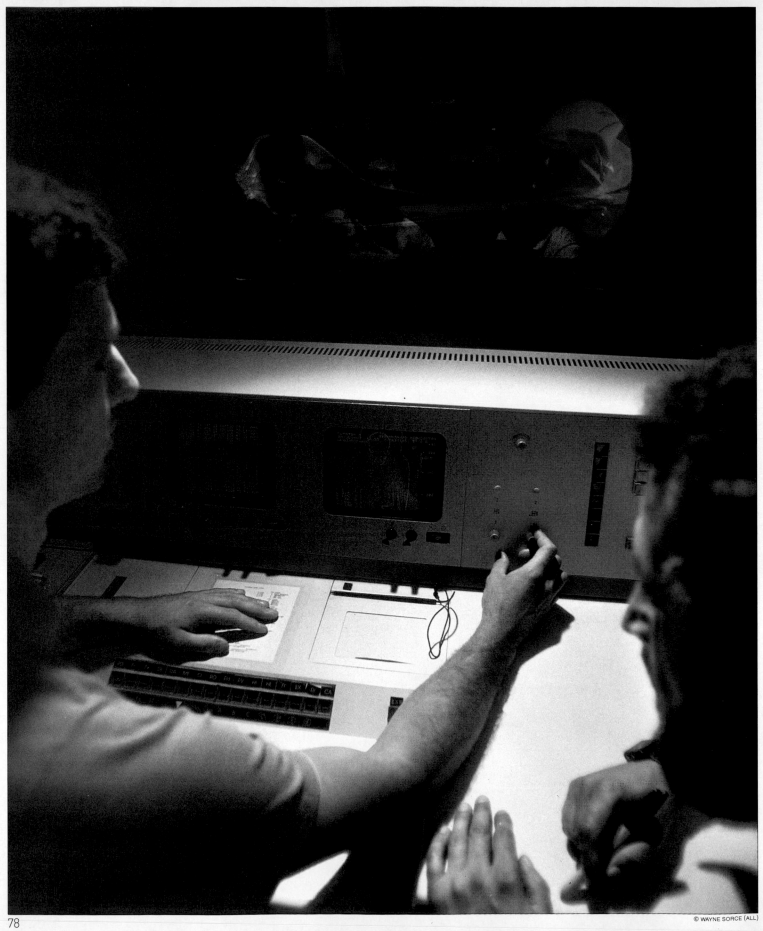

Experts at a Boston hospital use a CT scanner, or computerized X-ray machine, to examine a mummy inside an Egyptian burial case (left). The mummy is the remains of an Egyptian named Ankh-pef-hor. He lived sometime between 664 and 30 B.C., and he was buried in a brightly painted coffin (right). Without disturbing the fragile case, scientists discovered through CT (for computerized tomography) scans that the man was strong, and that he died young of unknown causes.

Skull and shoulders of Ankh-pef-hor's skeleton appear in an X ray (below, left). Scientists used the image as a guide while they produced CT scans like the one on the right, below. To get an idea of what that image shows, pretend that you're looking at the top of the mummy's head using X-ray vision. The two circles on either side of the head are the arms. The small ovals above the spine are chambers of the heart. Wavy lines represent cloth wrappings around the mummy's body; bright lines at the outer edge are the case. For this study, the CT scan will make a picture like this every 1/3 inch (8 mm), from head to toe.

(Continued from page 75) coffin in any way. Ankh-pef-hor had lain in the Boston Museum of Fine Arts since 1872. No one had opened his coffin for fear of destroying it. Ankh-pef-hor's mummy is one of several from the Boston collection that have been examined with the machine. People who work in museums in other cities also use CT scanners to unlock the secrets of the past. "The CT scan helps us learn about the process of mummification, and also about ancient diseases," says Dr. Myron Marx, who has worked with the mummy collection at the Boston museum.

Studying the past is an important job, and CT scanners are proving to be useful tools for archaeologists. Scanners help with museum studies only during slow periods at hospitals, however. The rest of the time, doctors use the machines to help them determine the condition of certain patients so they can decide on proper treatment.

Computers help doctors in other ways, too. Some can be programmed to aid in deciding what illness a person may have. One medical program, called HELP, stores in its memory the symptoms of many different diseases. After a patient's medical history is entered, HELP automatically keeps track of any medicines or lab tests the patient receives and any notes doctors or nurses take about the patient's condition. It then analyzes all the information. It alerts a doctor if one medicine might not combine well with another, if a dosage may be too large, or if the patient may have an allergic reaction. The program also suggests tests to run in order to gather more information about the

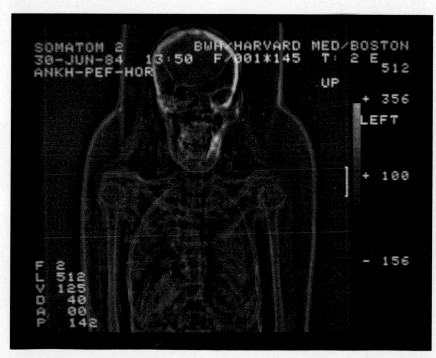

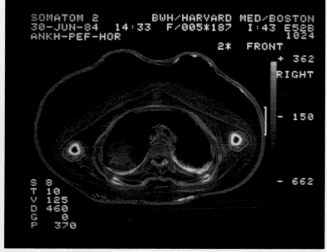

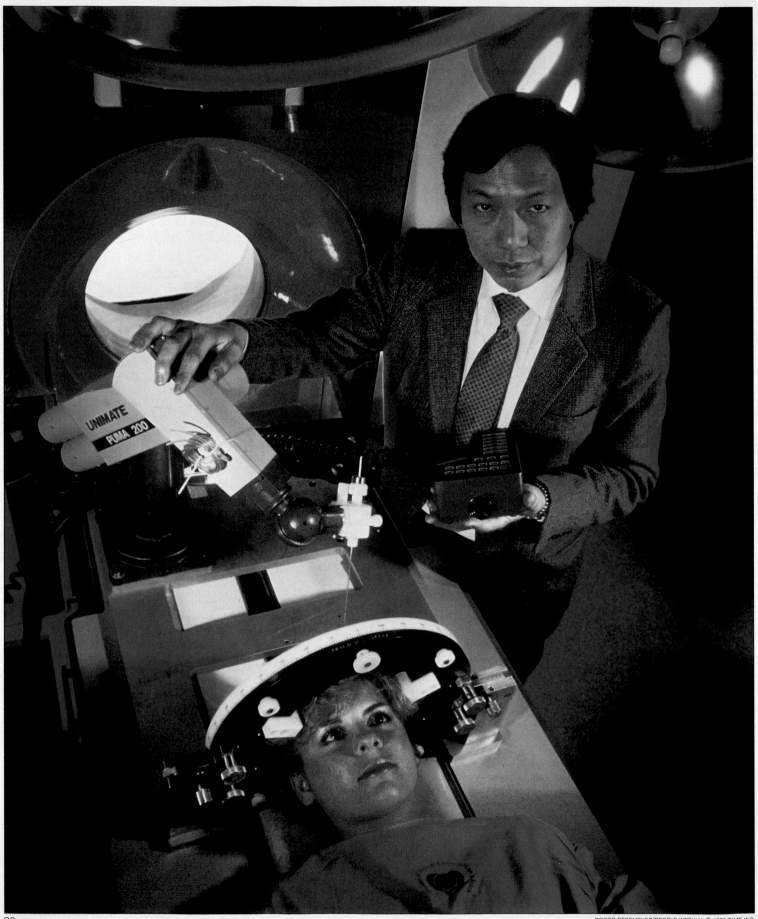

Surgeon's helper. Dr. Yik San Kwoh (left) invented OLE, a robotic brain surgeon. Here, he shows off key parts of his system—a programmable robotic arm and its control unit. A model plays the part of a patient with a possible brain problem. Here's how the system works. With the patient in place, specialists take CT scans of the patient's brain. After studying the scans, a doctor selects the safest path to the problem area. Then, at the doctor's order, the arm locks into position for the operation. The doctor then places different surgical instruments in a guide hole in the arm. With OLE to help, a doctor can perform extremely accurate surgery.

Electrodes dot the chest of a patient at a Minnesota hospital (below). They're hooked to a monitor that keeps track of the man's heart rate over a 24-hour period. A computer analyzes the information. This test is part of a study comparing the heart rhythms of twins growing up apart.

patient. A system like HELP is useful in enabling a doctor to confirm an opinion about a case and in suggesting other possible diagnoses that may have been overlooked. It's also a good study tool for medical students, who can compare their knowledge and conclusions with those of the computer.

Computers will never take the place of the human beings who work in hospitals—but the machines can be very helpful. Computers help doctors and nurses monitor patients. Computers attached to special equipment in intensive care units can print out an ongoing record of a patient's temperature, blood pressure, and pulse. Computers keep lists of what medicines the sick person has taken, and when each one was taken. These automatic medical histories save doctors and nurses valuable time.

In some hospitals, computers are even beginning to move into operating rooms. OLE, a robotic arm, acts as an extension of a surgeon's hand as the surgeon removes samples of brain tissue for study. OLE may be adapted for delicate surgery on injured knees. OLE

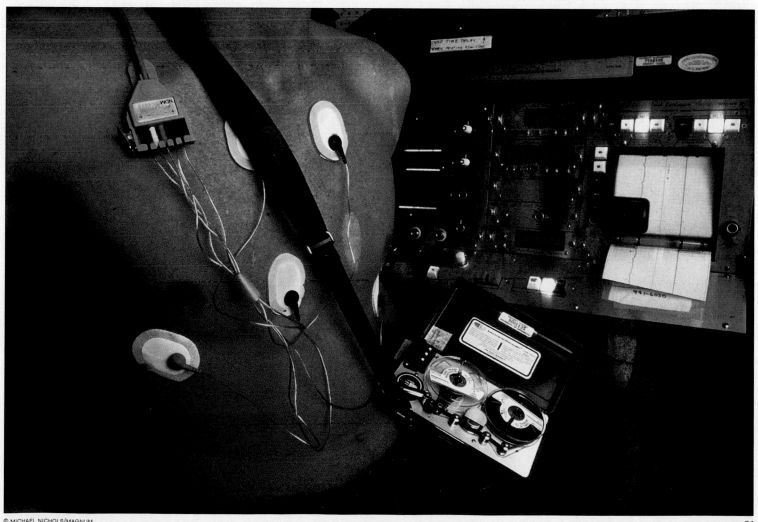

At sunrise on April 12, 1981, the space shuttle Columbia waits on its launch pad at Cape Canaveral, Florida (left). The shuttle takes off like a rocket, orbits like a spacecraft, and lands like an airplane. It would be out of business without computers. The machines run its entire flight system.

Later that morning, Columbia makes history as it streaks through the sky spitting steam and flame (below). Back on the ground, National Aeronautics and Space Administration scientists track the flight on computers.

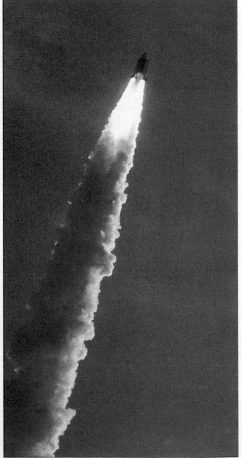

is the first computerized surgical robot—but don't be surprised if more robotic surgical equipment is available soon.

In hospitals, doctors depend on computers to help save lives. During space flights, astronauts rely on computers to run the support systems they need to stay alive, and to get them safely home to earth.

When the space shuttle lifts off, and throughout its mission, banks of computers aboard the craft keep track of how things are going. At the same time, powerful high-speed computers at Mission Control back on earth do their part to keep the flight on course. All these computers help control and monitor every part of a space flight, from the moment a craft leaves the launching pad until it reenters the earth's atmosphere and lands. At critical times during a shuttle flight, on-board computers perform 325,000 calculations a second.

The invention of computers made possible space flight as we know it today. Without the machines, human scientists just wouldn't have enough time to do all the calculations involved in a shuttle mission or other space flight.

Before the astronauts actually pilot the shuttle into space, they learn about the craft's equipment by practicing in a simulator, or working mock-up. The space shuttle simulator is no cheap imitation. It cost a hundred million dollars to build, and contains 12 computers. It gives astronauts-in-training a realistic experience of the sights and sounds of space flight.

Occasionally scientists send spacecraft on missions so long and so hazardous that human beings couldn't survive them. During the late 1970s, two

Astronaut Charles F. Bolden, Jr., left, and NASA employee Steve Nesbitt reach for control switches in a mock-up of the shuttle cockpit (below). Used for training, the model contains the same equipment used on real flights.

Rings of Saturn (left) show up clearly in a photograph sent back to earth from the Voyager II space probe. The rings actually are slightly different shades of yellow. Computers made them easier to see by changing some shades of yellow to other colors. Orbiting particles form the rings.

At NASA's Jet Propulsion Laboratory (JPL), in Pasadena, California (below), banks of computers help engineers keep an eye on spacecraft. JPL is part of a worldwide network that maintains a 24-hour watch. Screens on the lab wall show a map of the world, left, an image of Saturn's rings, center, and a list of the vehicles the lab is tracking. Computers at JPL record information sent back from spacecraft far away in the solar system. They record massive amounts of data that can be studied later.

Voyager space probes left earth, never to return. Since then, they have traveled more than a billion miles. Through the use of on-board computers, they have sent back millions of pieces of information about the planets they have passed on their journey out of our solar system.

Computers aboard the automated Voyagers gather and transmit data from space. Additional computers at NASA's Jet Propulsion Laboratory, in California, handle the data they send. A worldwide tracking system keeps a 24-hour watch on the Voyagers, as well as on other automated craft out in the solar system.

As the Voyager space probes passed Saturn, they made more than 30,000 photographs similar to the one at left. Scientists will be busy for years analyzing these and the masses of other data the Voyagers have collected. To do the job, scientists use computers. They also use computers to track the Voyagers'

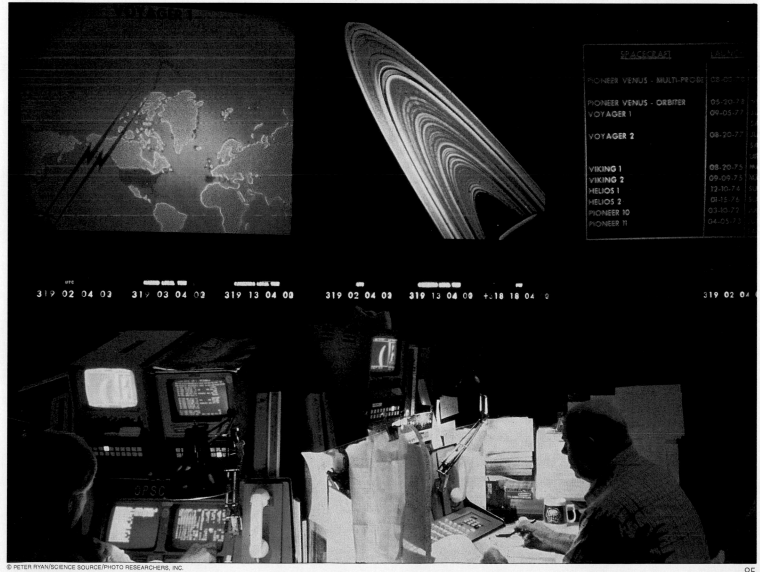

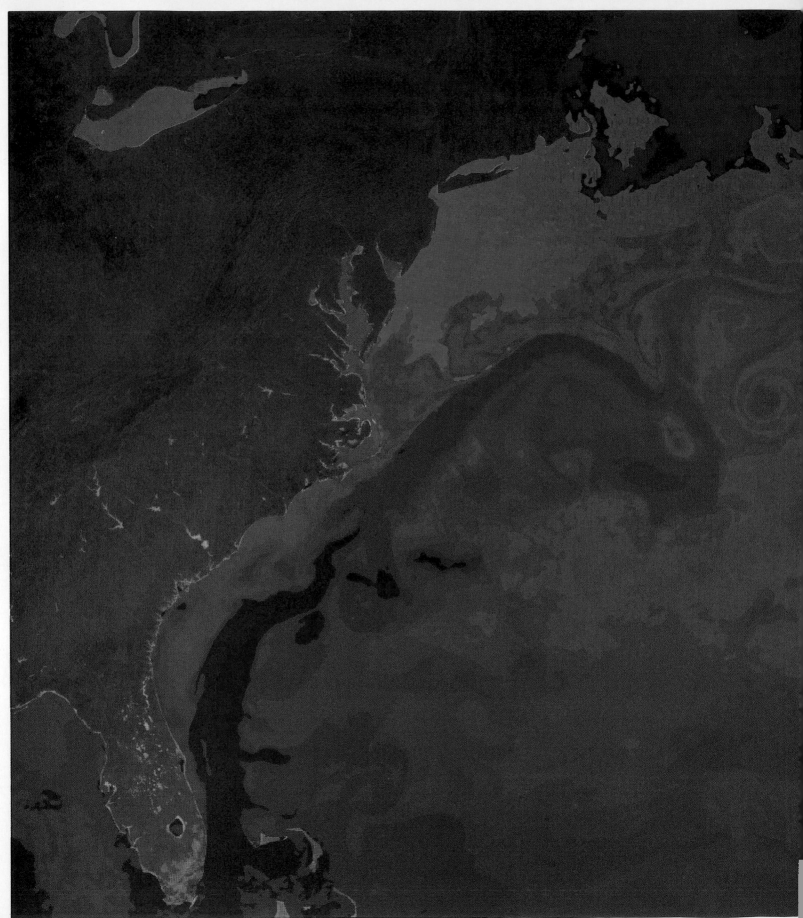

Color key to water temperatures
in the Atlantic Ocean*

■	37°F (3°C)		63°F (17°C)
■	48°F (9°C)		72°F (22°C)
■	55°F (13°C)	■	81°F (27°C)

*These figures have been rounded off.

journeys—and will keep up the watch until the end of the 20th century and possibly into the 21st.

The Voyager missions have taught scientists a lot about distant parts of the solar system. Other spacecraft have paid attention to a more familiar place— our own planet earth. Experts at the National Oceanic and Atmospheric Administration, known as NOAA, use satellites to gather all kinds of important information about the atmosphere and the earth.

Placed in orbit around the earth, NOAA satellites aim heat-sensing scanners at the surface below. The map on the left was made with such a scanner. The scanner beamed coded information about the varying temperatures in the ocean to computers on earth. Computers, under the direction of experts, changed the code into images, and added color to show the differences in temperature.

Scientists at NOAA work for the U. S. Government. They're in charge of gathering scientific data about the ocean, the atmosphere, space, and the sun, and about the nation's coastal waters, Great Lakes, and navigable rivers. Some of the data is used by the National Ocean Service, an agency of NOAA that makes and publishes charts of the coastal waters and information about ocean tides and currents. NOAA satellites and computers also furnish images to another of its agencies, the National Weather Service, to help predict what our weather will be. You may see NOAA computer maps made from satellite data when you

Color codes reveal different temperatures in the Atlantic Ocean along the eastern coast of North America (left). This map was formed from 40 photographs that a National Oceanic and Atmospheric Administration satellite sent back to earth during June 1984. Under the direction of specialists, computers put the pictures together and added the colors. On this map, the coldest currents are colored magenta. The warmest ones show up as red. Temperatures between register as purple, blue, green, and yellow. From maps like these, scientists learn much about our planet's temperature and weather patterns.

tune in your local TV news show to find out if there's rain in the forecast.

In just about any scientific laboratory you might visit today, you would see computer terminals, keyboards, and screens in use. In the picture below, two technicians work in a lab filled with computer equipment at NASA's National Transonic Facility, in Hampton, Virginia. These technicians are working with a design for a high-speed jet. To see just how the jet would behave in actual wind conditions, they experiment with a scale-model airplane inside a wind tunnel. They control the wind speeds inside the tunnel with a computer-controlled fan. Once the experiment has been completed, scientists will use computers to analyze the results of the wind tunnel test.

For most scientists—whether they study the oceans, the solar system, or the inside of the human body—the computer is as familiar as the test tube, the telescope, or the microscope. Even to nonscientists, computers are becoming more familiar every day. How will computers affect our lives in the years to come? For a peek into the future, turn the page.

A scale model of an advanced transport aircraft undergoes tests at NASA's National Transonic Facility, in Hampton, Virginia (right). This facility, a computerized wind tunnel, enables technicians to conduct flight tests in miniature. In this test, a 50-inch-long (127-cm) model performs just as a full-size plane would while flying at 600 miles an hour (965 km/hr)—approaching the speed of sound. The wind tunnel can simulate, or imitate, wind conditions of more than 800 miles an hour (1287 km/h). The red coloring comes from a filter on the photographer's flash.

In the control room, technicians run a flight test (below). The technician on the left sets the model plane's angle in relation to the ground. The other technician controls wind speed and other forces in the tunnel. He makes the conditions inside as close as possible to the ones that planes actually meet at high speeds and high altitudes. A computer will record the results. The data will help in designing new airplanes and in improving existing ones.

COMPUTING THE FUTURE

Xanadu (ZAN-uh-du), a futuristic home, stands near Orlando, Florida. To shape the house, Xanadu's builders sprayed plastic foam over huge balloons. When the foam hardened, they peeled away the balloons. In the future, many homes will have central computers that will control lights and appliances. Computers also will work the heating and cooling systems, check security, and watch for fire.

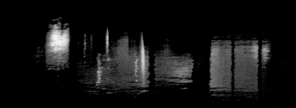

KEVIN FLEMING

It's early morning. The sun is barely up, but the brain of your computerized house is already hard at work. To prepare for breakfast, the central computer directs automatic kitchen appliances to make hot drinks and to heat the food that is waiting in the oven. It warms your shower water to your favorite temperature, then uses a synthesized voice to wake you gently from a sound sleep. The computer doesn't have to ask how you feel today. It knows. During the night, sensors in your bed checked your pulse and your temperature and reported the results to the central computer.

You stumble into the shower. Once you're refreshed and wide awake, you stand in front of your automatic clothes retrieval unit. The conveyor system in this computerized closet brings your clean, pressed clothes into reach, and you get dressed. Just before you go to meet with your electronic tutor, you check in with the computer one more time. It reminds you that you're playing in a soccer game in the afternoon.

After your soccer game, you return home and find the door locked. You ask it to unlock itself, and it does.

The central computer recognized your voice and ordered the door to open.

This sounds like a dream or a movie, doesn't it? In computerized homes of the future, however, things like this may go on every day.

Xanadu, a house outside Orlando, Florida, shows what some people think the home of tomorrow may be like. From the outside, Xanadu looks like something from another planet. It is made of hardened plastic foam that was sprayed onto huge balloons to form rooms. The inside of Xanadu is even more futuristic than the outside. Computers attached to dozens of electronic gadgets run everything.

No one lives in Xanadu, but many visitors go there to peek at the computerized home of the future.

Comfortable computing. During a visit to Xanadu, Tammi Ludwig, 7, on the left, and Hope Holland, 8, both of Kissimmee, Florida, tap away on a computer keyboard as they sit on a round bed (below). In the home of the future, people may be able to control coffeepots and front door locks from their bedrooms.

Following an electronic tour guide, they see the constantly changing computer-graphics art show on video screens in the family room. They learn in the master bedroom about the security and fire systems. They visit the master bath where a bather can enjoy a sun-heated steam bath or choose from a variety of computer-produced weather conditions.

Many visitors to Xanadu think the house is an exciting idea. One such visitor was 9-year-old Katie Steinmetz, of Barrington, Illinois, shown in the photograph below. "She would have moved in the next day," her mother reports.

Many of the computer devices that Xanadu shows off are still only in the planning stage. Even so, it's reasonable to think they will be used someday.

Katie Steinmetz, 9, of Barrington, Illinois, and her mother play in the family room (below). Video screens and other electronic equipment cover the walls. Xanadu's builders call the entertainment center an "electronic hearth." They planned it as a gathering place for families—just as a fireplace hearth is.

Already, builders are equipping new houses with computer systems that turn the lights on and off and adjust heating and cooling. One company has developed a computerized watering system for lawns. The device measures the moisture in the soil and turns on sprinklers when the soil can best absorb the water.

The home of the future often will be the office of the future. When you are older, you might get a job using computers—but you might not have to go to an office every day. Instead, you might work at a computer terminal in your home. You'd communicate with your fellow workers by using a video screen.

If you do go to the office of the future, you're likely to find that it, too, has been changed by computers. Some experts think that one day typing—a common activity at many businesses—will have disappeared. Instead, a computerized typewriter without a keyboard will be able to hear voices, take dictation, and print out clean copies of letters, reports, or stories. Such machines might be called "talkwriters."

If your future job takes you into a factory, you'll probably find that changed, too. Robots may have

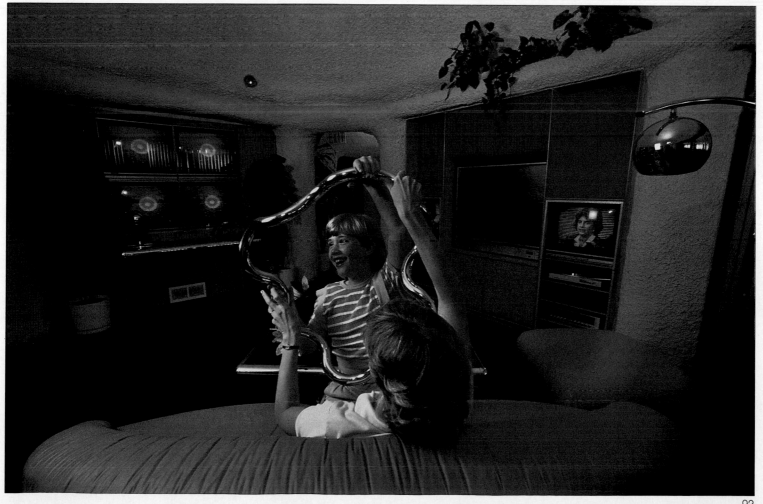

94

been put to work doing many jobs now done by humans. This will free the humans to do more varied or less dangerous work. Look at the factory in the photograph on the left. The Japanese government built the plant, which manufactured automotive parts, as an experiment. The picture looks as if it were made after the place had shut down for the weekend. Actually, the factory seemed this deserted most days. Even so, work went on—performed by computer-controlled machines, lasers, and robots.

In the future, engineers are likely to build robots that can do even complicated work. The IBM Corporation produces a robot called the model 7565. This robot can pick up an egg and handle it without breaking the shell. This may not be an especially useful thing for a machine to do—but it's a big step forward in robot technology. Now that robots can perform such delicate tasks, they can do much more than just weld car bodies together or hold paint sprayers or move parts from place to place.

ODEX I, the spiderlike robot on the right, adapts itself to many jobs. Guided by an operator using a joystick, it moves heavy objects and climbs up and down. ODEX I is flexible. It can stretch to peer over things with its camera eyes. It can squat to get through low tunnels or under obstacles. Future models of ODEX I, and other computerized robots like it, will be able to perform difficult, dangerous jobs in environments where people would rather not work. They will explore parched deserts and icy ocean depths. They may even visit cold, empty planets in distant space.

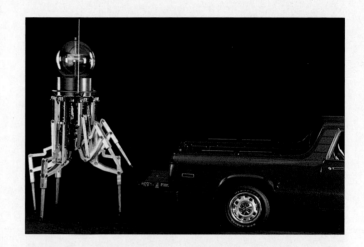

Future factory. "Workers" at this factory in Tsukuba Science City, in Japan (left), turned out gearboxes for cars—and they did it with little human help. The factory, built as an experiment and now closed, was operated mostly by computers and robots. Human workers watched over the plant, but they did no physical tasks. Factories like this one will probably produce goods in the future.

Climb aboard. A robot named ODEX I climbs into the back of a pickup truck (right). The six-legged robot is strong enough to lift the back end of the truck off the ground and pull it along. Future generations of ODEX will be able to walk and work almost anywhere—from the seafloor to the surfaces of distant planets.

The engineers who make ODEX I think the robot could also be useful on farms of the future. What might those farms be like? One way to find out is to visit The Land, an exhibit area and research station at Walt Disney World's Epcot Center.

In The Land's huge greenhouses, agricultural experts grow foods adapted to different climates, from very dry to very wet. Each crop grows best under certain conditions. Computers play a role in keeping the indoor climates just right. They keep track of the temperature and humidity. They even measure the amount of moisture on the surface of the plants' leaves. Using the computer's information, people adjust some of the conditions in each greenhouse to produce the best results. Other computers monitor the environment in tanks where fish are raised for food.

You'll have many professions to choose from in the future. Whether you work at a newspaper or in an office, on a farm or in a *(Continued on page 101)*

Gone fishing. At Walt Disney World's Epcot Center, near Orlando, Florida, Jane Evans prepares to scoop a fish from an aquaculture tank in The Land pavilion (right), an exhibition area devoted to agriculture. Computers monitor the quality of the water in which the fish grow. They also record how much the fish eat and how much they grow. Fish harvested from this tank will be served at The Land's revolving restaurant.

Computerized farming methods at The Land help scientist Gary Paul grow lettuce (below). The sensor panel on the left monitors the temperature, the humidity, and the light in the greenhouse. The panel sends the information to a central computer in another building. Experts make adjustments so that conditions in the greenhouse are always ideal for growing lettuce.

Untangling the problems of
a supercomputer keeps a specialist
called a "checkout engineer" busy.
He's giving the system its final test.
This engineer works with more than
65 miles (105 km) of wire inside a
CYBER 205. To get at the complex
electronic system, the engineer
removed the computer's back panel.
The loops of wire carry electronic
signals at about 150,000 miles a
second (241,350 km/s). That's four-
fifths the speed of light. Information
traveling at that speed could move
through the 65-mile network in less
than a second!

Robots of all shapes and sizes crowd around robotics expert Deb Huglin (left). She holds a computer-controlled robotic arm. In front of her are smaller robots that flash, whir, and turn. Most of these robots are only toys. In the future, however, robots may be our helpers, protectors, and companions.

"Vid Kid" Rawson Stovall, of Abilene, Texas, demonstrates a computer at the 1984 Bits & Bytes exhibit, in Anaheim, California (below). Charles Morton, 16, of Wilmington, California, center, and Sam Ledwitz, 14, of San Gabriel, California, watch closely. At Bits & Bytes, visitors tried out many kinds of computers. Rawson, 14, delivered a speech at the show. When it comes to computers, the Vid Kid should know what he's talking about. He reviews both software and hardware in a weekly column carried by four newspapers. Rawson started the column in 1982. A collection of his columns has been published as a book: The Vid Kid's Book of Home Video Games.

(Continued from page 96) factory, you will probably use computers in one way or another. Of course, there's one business in which you're guaranteed to use the amazing machines: the computer business.

Experts at the United States Department of Labor say that most of the fastest-growing occupations today involve computers. Some people write programs, while others design and build the hardware to run them. Some make their living repairing or selling computers. And some—like 14-year-old Rawson Stovall, of Abilene, Texas—keep up with the computer industry and write about it. Rawson, who calls himself the "Vid Kid," has written a newspaper column about computers for several years.

Rawson became interested in computers as a third grader, when he discovered video games. Since then, he has reviewed hundreds of programs and learned a lot about computers. What does he think his future in the computer world will be like? "I've seen so many advances since I've been writing my column that I believe I'll be using computers in ways and for things that I can't even imagine now."

INDEX

Bold type indicates illustrations; regular type refers to text.

EDUCATIONAL CONSULTANTS

Rachelle S. Heller, Ph.D., Department of Electrical Engineering and Computer Science, The George Washington University, *Chief Consultant*
Glenn O. Blough, LL.D., Emeritus Professor of Education, University of Maryland, *Educational Consultant*
Barbara J. Wood, Montgomery County (Maryland) Public Schools, *Reading Consultant*
Nicholas J. Long, Ph.D., *Consulting Psychologist*

The Special Publications and School Services Division is grateful to the individuals and organizations named or quoted in the text and to those cited here for their generous cooperation and assistance during the preparation of COMPUTERS, THOSE AMAZING MACHINES:
   Sue D'Auria, Boston Museum of Fine Arts; Catholic University; Alfred I. DuPont Institute; Federal Reserve Bank; General Micro Computer; Steven K. Knapp, Intel Corporation; Los Alamos National Laboratory; New York City Police Department; Tyler Vision Program, D. C. Schools.

ADDITIONAL READING

Readers may want to check the *National Geographic Index* and the *World Index* in a school or a public library for related articles and to refer to the following books.
   ("A" indicates a book for readers at adult level.)

Ardley, Neil, *Computers*, Warwick, 1983. Augarten, Stan, *Bit by Bit*, Ticknor & Fields, 1984 (A). Ball, Marion J., *What is a Computer?*, Houghton Mifflin, 1972. Bowe, Frank G., *Personal Computers & Special Needs*, Sybex, Inc., 1984 (A). Chester, Michael, *Robots, Facts Behind the Fiction*, MacMillan Publishing Company, 1983 (A). *Computer Basics*, Time-Life Books, 1985 (A). Gallagher, Sharon, *Inside the Personal Computer (A Pop-Up Guide)*, Abbeville Press, Inc., 1984. Hawkes, Nigel, *Computers, How They Work*, Franklin Watts, 1983. Heller, Rachelle S., and C. Dianne Martin, *Bits 'n Bytes About Computing: A Computer Literacy Primer*, Computer Science Press, 1982. Mason, Roy, with Lane Jennings and Robert Evans, *Xanadu*, Acropolis, 1984. Smith, Brian Reffin, *Computers*, Usborne Publishing, 1981. Shurkin, Joel, *Engines of the Mind*, W. W. Norton & Company, 1984 (A). Tatchell, Judy, and Bill Bennett, *Usborne Guide to Understanding the Micro*, Usborne Publishing, 1982. Weber, Jack, *Computers, the Next Generation*, Arco, 1985.

Composition for COMPUTERS, THOSE AMAZING MACHINES by National Geographic's Photographic Services, Carl M. Shrader, Director; Lawrence F. Ludwig, Assistant Director. Printed and bound by Holladay-Tyler Printing Corp., Rockville, Md. Color Separations by the Lanman-Progressive Co., Washington, D. C.; Lincoln Graphics, Inc., Cherry Hill, N. J.; NEC, Inc., Nashville, Tenn.

Library of Congress CIP Data
O'Neill, Catherine, 1950-
      Computers, those amazing machines.
      (Books for world explorers)
      Bibliography: p.
      Includes index.
      Summary: Examines the history, functions, and influences of computers in everyday life, science, and discusses careers in the field.
      1. Computers—Juvenile literature. [1. Computers]
I. Title.   II. Series.
QA76.23.O54   1985   004   85-25905
ISBN 0-87044-574-X (regular edition)
ISBN 0-87044-579-0 (library edition)

COMPUTERS
THOSE AMAZING MACHINES

by Catherine O'Neill

PUBLISHED BY
THE NATIONAL GEOGRAPHIC SOCIETY
WASHINGTON, D.C.

Gilbert M. Grosvenor, *President*
Melvin M. Payne, *Chairman of the Board*
Owen R. Anderson, *Executive Vice President*
Robert L. Breeden, *Senior Vice President, Publications and Educational Media*

PREPARED BY THE SPECIAL PUBLICATIONS
AND SCHOOL SERVICES DIVISION

Donald J. Crump, *Director*
Philip B. Silcott, *Associate Director*
William L. Allen, *Assistant Director*

BOOKS FOR WORLD EXPLORERS
Pat Robbins, *Editor*
Ralph Gray, *Editor Emeritus*
Margaret McKelway, *Associate Editor*
Ursula Perrin Vosseler, *Art Director*

STAFF FOR *COMPUTERS*
Margaret McKelway, *Managing Editor*
Charles M. Kogod, *Picture Editor*
Lynette R. Ruschak, *Art Director*
M. Linda Lee, Barbara A. Payne, *Researchers*
Lucinda Moore, *Contributing Researcher*
John F. Porter, *Artist*
Patricia N. Holland, *Special Projects Editor*
Lori Elizabeth Davie, *Editorial Assistant*
Bernadette L. Grigonis, *Illustrations Assistant*

ENGRAVING, PRINTING, AND PRODUCT MANUFACTURE: Robert W. Messer, *Manager;* David V. Showers, *Production Manager;* Gregory Storer, *Production Project Manager;* Mark R. Dunlevy, George J. Zeller, Jr., *Assistant Production Managers;* Timothy H. Ewing, *Production Assistant;* Kevin P. Heubusch, *Production Staff Assistant*

STAFF ASSISTANTS: Dianne T. Craven, Carol R. Curtis, Mary Elizabeth Davis, Ann Di Fiore, Rosamund Garner, Virginia W. Hannasch, Nancy J. Harvey, Joan Hurst, Linda Johnson, Katherine R. Leitch, Ann E. Newman, Cleo Petroff, Stuart E. Pfitzinger, Pamela Black Townsend, Virginia A. Williams, Eric Wilson

MARKET RESEARCH: Mark W. Brown, Joseph S. Fowler, Carrla L. Holmes, Meg M. Keiffer, Barbara Steinwurtzel, Marsha Sussman, Judy Turnbull

INDEX: James B. Enzinna